THE CRISIS OF DISSENT

Gerard Morrissey

L.C. Classification Number: BX1407.H4M67
ISBN: 0-931888-19-0

NIHIL OBSTAT:
  Rev. Msgr. Richard J. Burke, V. G.

IMPRIMATUR:
  Rev. Msgr. Richard J. Burke
  Vicar General
  Diocese of Arlington
  April 26, 1985

The *nihil obstat* and *imprimatur* are official declarations that a book or pamphlet is free of doctrinal or moral error. No implication is contained therein that those who have granted the *nihil obstat* and *imprimatur* agree with the contents, opinions, or statements expressed.

To My Mother and Father

Christendom Publishing Group

CONTENTS

Publishing Group Members, continued.

Mr. & Mrs. Dennis P. McEneany
Mr. J. R. McMahon
Mrs. Kenneth McNichol
Dr. & Mrs. H. W. Meid
Reverend Robert A. Meng
Dr. & Mrs. Patrick A. Metress
Mr. Philip L. Metschan
Mr. & Mrs. Larry Miggins
Mr. Joseph Monahan
Reverend Hugh Monmonier
Mr. James B. Mooney
Mrs. Gertrude G. Moore
Mr. Robert E. Morey
Col. Chester H. Morneau
Mr. Leo Mount
Mr. Nicholas J. Mulhall
Mr. Charles J. Murach
Mrs. Rita Murphy
Mr. & Mrs. G. W. Muth
Mr. L. Maxwell Narby
Mr. Frank C. Nelick
Mr. Frank Newlin
Mr. Paul O'Connell
Mr. Richard J. O'Donnell
Maj. Michael J. O'Hara USMC
Mr. Chris T. O'Keefe
Mr. John F. O'Shaughnessy Jr.
Mrs. Josephine Kline Ogden
Miss Veronica M. Oravec
Mrs. John F. Parker
Mr. Ernest Patry
Reverend Angelo Patti
Brother Stephen F. Paul
Rev. Mr. Laszlo S. Pavel
Mr. Joseph Pearce
Mr. & Mrs. Joseph (Mary) Peek
Bill and Mary Peffley
Mr. Alfred H. Pekarek
Robert N. Pelaez M.D.
Mr. John H. Pelletier
Mrs. Cherylyn Pentecost
Mrs. Angela M. Peters
Mr. & Mrs. C. J. Petrovits
Mr. & Mrs. Gerald R. Pfeiffer
Mr. & Mrs. Pat Pollock
Mr. & Mrs. William H. Power Jr.
Dr. & Mrs. Charles P. Prezzia
Mr. Stuart Quinlan
Mrs. Mary F. Quinn
Mr. Thomas J. Quinn
Mr. & Mrs. Joseph E. Rau
Reverend Robert A. Reed
Mrs. John F. Reid
Mr. & Mrs. John J. Reuter
Msgr. William J. Reynolds
Dr. Charles E. Rice
Dr. & Mrs. Robert C. Rice
M. V. Rock M.D.
Brother Philip Romano OFMCap
Mr. Bernard J. Ruby
Mr. Mark V. Ruessmann

Miss Agnes J. Ryan
Mr. Thomas J. Sanko
Mr. Richard W. Sassman
Mr. Edward F. Scanlon
Mr. & Mrs. George Scanlon
Miss Marian C. Schatzman
Miss Constance M. Scheetz
Mrs. Margaret Scheetz
Mr. Peter Scheetz
Mrs. Francis R. Schirra
Mrs. Claragene Schmidt
Mr. & Mrs. Ralph Schutzman
Mr. Frank P. Scrivener
Mr. & Mrs. Robert K. Scrivener
John B. Shea
John R. Sheehan M.D.
Miss Anne Sherman
Mr. & Mrs. John Shumski
Mrs. Bernice Simon
Mr. Richard M. Sinclair, Jr.
Mrs. Patricia L. Singletary
Major Arthur Sippo
Mrs. Walter Skorupski
Mrs. Joan M. Smith
Miss Mary Carole Smith
Mr. William Smith
Mr. & Mrs. William M. Smith
Miss Ann Spalding
Mr. & Mrs. James Spargo
Mr. John S. Steffen
Miss Anne M. Stinnett
Miss Sylvia H. Stokes
Mr. Michael Sullivan
Mr. John Svarc
Mr. Edward S. Szymanski
Mr. Edward B. Timko
Mr. Richard J. Titus
Mr. Dominic Torlone
Reverend Christopher Twohig
Mr. Michael Vachon
Mr. & Mrs. Albert Vallone
Mr. Willem Van Achthoven
Miss Alice Vandenberg
Reverend Frederick J. Vaughn
Mr. Csaba Vedlik, Jr.
Dr. John w. Vincent
Mr. William C. Vinet, Jr.
Mrs. Catherine Wahlmeier
Mr. David P. Walkey
General Vernon A. Walters
Mrs. Alice V. Ward
Mr. Fulton John Waterloo
P. S. Weinert Family
Mr. Ralph A. Wellings
Mr. Leonard N. Weydert, Jr.
Miss Penny Wiest
John R. Wilhelmy, D.D.S.
Mrs. Mary Williams
Mr. Michael C. Wimm
Mrs. Marguerite A. Wright

Introduction

This is the second of three books written for Catholics who wish to defend the official teaching of the Church. As stated in the introduction to the first book (*Defending the Papacy*), each of the three books concentrates on a specific question. The three questions are:

1) What is the official teaching of the Church?

(Discussed in Book One—*Defending the Papacy*)

2) If, as the Apostolic Delegate's letter indicates, many Church institutions in the United States are undermining this teaching and harming the faith, then how did the present situation develop and why have those attacking the Church from within made such progress?

(Discussed in This Book)

3) What steps can be taken by Catholics loyal to the Pope both to safeguard their own faith (and the faith of their children) and to strengthen respect for the Church's teaching authority within the Catholic community in our country?

(To be discussed in Book Three)

In the first book, we considered the official teaching of the Church. There were extensive quotations from the Popes and from Church Councils to illustrate this teaching. We also discussed a few of the tricks used by Church dissenters in their attempt to undermine the confidence of Catholics in the Pope.

Now we move on to a somewhat different question. In spite of the fact that Vatican II strongly reasserted traditional Catholic teaching, the power of Church dissenters seems to have grown remarkably since Vatican II. This did not happen by accident. What strategies were employed by Church dissenters to advance their position?

At first glance the odds would seem to be much against the dissenters. The official Church teaching strongly disagrees with them. The Pope disagrees with them. The overwhelming majority of the bishops are on the public record as disagreeing with them. Thousands of priests, religious, and laity also disagree with them.

Nevertheless, despite these factors, it is often the orthodox Catholics—and not the dissenters—who feel frustrated. Loyal Catholics—whether they are laity, priests, or even bishops—keep saying that somebody else should act (usually the Church authority directly above them) but feel powerless to do anything themselves to counteract the dissenters. Rarely have so few terrorized so many.

Why study such a depressing situation? Such a study is necessary for one reason. If orthodox Catholics are to win their all-important struggle to defend the Church's teaching, we must understand clearly the reasons for the current success of the dissenters as well as the reasons why loyal Catholics often feel powerless. Based upon this knowledge, we must then devise an effective plan of action. In any contest, the key to victory is to study closely the strategy of one's opponents—and then, having done so, to prepare and execute a better strategy of one's own.

1.
Two Cardinals and Two Bishops

A good way to begin our consideration of the present crisis is to look at five statements made since Vatican II by Cardinals and Archbishops; two by Archbishop Fulton Sheen, and one each by Cardinal John Wright, Cardinal Francis Seper, and Archbishop Pio Laghi.¹ Two of the quotations have been cited already in our first volume, but they are repeated here to give us a full picture of the current situation.

(1)   The bishops, who obtained many powers for themselves at the Council, are often to blame because in this crisis they are not exercising their powers as they should. Rome is too far away to cope with every scandal—and Rome is not well obeyed. If all the bishops would deal decisively with these aberrations as they occur, the situation would be different. It is very difficult for us in Rome if we get no cooperation from the bishops.
               —*Cardinal Francis Seper (Prefect of the Congregation*
                              for the Doctrine of the Faith)

(2)   The great danger to be avoided in the new catechetics is that of the excessive 'professionalism'—enormous 'know how' and meager 'know what' and 'know why,' at least so far as Christian doctrine is concerned. It is a danger so well verified in some places that parents have pulled, as if from the burning, their children from the hands of the mere professional religious educators.
—*Cardinal John Wright (Prefect of the Congregation for the Clergy)*

(3)   With increasing frequency the Holy See receives letters from the United States complaining about articles appearing in Catholic newspapers, including diocesan publications, which cause harm to the

Faith of the people because of lack of respect for the teaching and decisions of the magisterium. As you know, it is not unusual for such articles to contain criticisms and attacks even on the teaching authority and the person of the Holy Father. The impact of such criticism is heightened when columns are syndicated and widely circulated.

A letter from the Secretariat of State (March 31, 1981; Protocol No. 63408) expressed concern over this problem, and ordinaries are encouraged to consider their responsibilities in governing the policies of those publications over which they have control. To this I would add a word of encouragement for the promotion of a sound and vital Catholic press, so useful an instrument for evangelization and so vibrant in the life of the Church in the United States.

—*Archbishop Pio Laghi (Apostolic Delegate to the United States)*

(4)   I tell my relatives and friends with college age children to send them to secular colleges where they will have to fight for their faith, rather than to Catholic colleges where it will be taken from them."

—*Archbishop Fulton Sheen*

(5)   When the Church is holy—that is to say, when we the members are holy. . . the opposition always comes from outside the Church—for example, in persecution. When the Church is not so holy, as it is now, then the opposition comes from within—from his [the Pope's] own. That is why he [Pope Paul VI] said his heart was broken."

—*Archbishop Fulton Sheen*

Cardinal Wright speaks of religious education programs. Archbishop Laghi speaks of Catholic newspapers. Archbishop Sheen speaks of Catholic colleges. Yet the message is the same—as operated today, these institutions can destroy the faith of Catholics.

How ironic it is to say that! The purpose of all these institutions is to strengthen the Catholic faith. That is the primary reason for their being. After all, an institution is simply an organization that is setup up to achieve a certain goal. Faced with the difficult responsibility of teaching the doctrine of Christ to every generation, the Church has brought these educational organizations into existence. Nevertheless, if the cardinals and archbishops are correct, the very institutions so established are now being used for exactly the opposite purpose. If the Cardinals and Archbishops are correct, and I believe they are, a warning out to be given to all Catholics who come into contact with these institutions—a caution similar to the one that appears on cigarette packages: "Warning: Reading this diocesan newspaper, participating in this parish-sponsored religious education program, attending this Catholic college, may be dangerous to your spiritual health and may even result in the loss of your faith."

Is that too strong? No stronger than the words of the cardinals and archbishops themselves. Archbishop Sheen puts it bluntly. You can lose your faith by going to a "Catholic" college. According to the Archbishop, you may even be safer at a secular college. Not that a secular college is friendly to Catholicism—but at least you know that fact when you go there. You will not be taken by surprise. At a Catholic college, on the other hand, you presume that you are among friends. You believe that the teachers are representatives of the Catholic Church and you trust them for that reason. Precisely because your defenses are down, your faith can be shattered in a way that is not possible at a secular college.

Cardinal Wright is no less blunt. He compares some religious education programs to a fire. Parents have to pull their children from this fire or they will die. And who set the fire? The professional educators trained and employed by the Catholic Church.

Perhaps the most surprising quote of all comes from Cardinal Seper. Speaking of contemporary difficulties in defending the Catholic faith, he says straightforwardly that it is the local bishops who "are to blame" for the present situation. Not that the local bishops are dissenters themselves but "they are not exercising their powers as they should . . . If all the bishops would deal decisively with these aberrations as they occur, the situation would be different."

Archbishop Laghi seems to be making a similar point in a more indirect way. He is writing to "ordinaries," those bishops appointed by the Pope to head the local dioceses. What is his message to the bishops? "Ordinaries are encouraged to consider their responsibilities in governing the policies of those publications over which they have control." The Archbishop also stresses that diocesan newspapers, the official publication of the local bishop, are among those periodicals carrying articles that ridicule the Pope and Catholic teaching. The implication is clear that some bishops are not exercising their powers as they should.

Archbishop Sheen, Cardinal Wright, Archbishop Laghi, and Cardinal Seper: These are high-ranking churchmen, but more than that, people with a special knowledge in the areas about which they were speaking. Archbishop Sheen was for many years a university professor who specialized in theology and philosophy; Cardinal Wright was appointed by the Holy Father to head the Sacred Congregation for the Clergy, a Vatican department that has the responsibility of carrying out the desires of the Pope with respect to catechetics and other forms of religious instruction; Cardinal Seper was appointed by the Holy Father to head the Sacred Congregation for the Doctrine of the Faith, a Vatican department to which the Pope has given the responsibility of safeguarding Church teaching on faith and morals; Archbishop Laghi is the official representative of the Pope to the Catholic Church in America, who makes it clear that what he is writing does not originate with him as a private opinion but is a directive that comes from Rome itself.

So what do we have? The American bishop with the most extensive experience in university life says that Catholic colleges are often a danger to the faith. The Cardinal appointed to supervise catechetics says the same thing with respect to catechetical programs. The Apostolic Delegate pleads with the local bishops to keep the official newspapers they publish from ridiculing the Pope and Catholic teaching, while the Cardinal appointed to lead the effort to safeguard faith and morals is convinced that the crisis is caused to a great extent by the failure of the local bishops to use their powers in defense of Church teaching.

If you or I had made comments similar to those of the cardinals and archbishops, the charge would probably be made that we were either ignorant or disloyal to the local bishop. That is the reason it is most important to keep in mind always that the questions we will be studying in this book are questions that have been raised by Rome itself. Therefore, it is not only permissible but necessary that loyal Catholics discuss these problems— because we must understand clearly what has gone wrong if we are ever to make things right.

There is one quotation from the cardinals and archbishops above that we have yet to consider. While the other four quotations tell us what is happening, this is the only quotation to tell us why. Archbishop Sheen explains that the Church is never without the Cross of Christ. In other words, she is always suffering in one way or another—always under attack from some quarter. Where the attack comes from, however, depends upon the holiness of the members of the Church. There is a sense in which the Church is always holy because Jesus, Mary, and the saints are always present to her. Nevertheless, because the individual Catholics living on earth have the freedom to accept or reject God's guidance in whole or in part, the members of the Church can vary greatly in holiness from age to age. According to Archbishop Sheen, in ages when the Church is holy the attack on her comes from without, for example in a persecution. In ages when the Church is not so holy, and the Archbishop believes ours is such an age, the attack comes from within. At such a time it is Catholics themselves who ridicule the Pope and sneer at Church teaching.

Archbishop Sheen's reference to "outside" and 'inside" reminds us that the current attacks on the Pope and on Catholic teaching are not new. The only new element is the place from which these attacks come.

To illustrate this, let us consider a book that was written a few years ago by a "Catholic theologian." Among the Church beliefs called into question by this particular dissenter were the following:

a)   the sacrificial value of Christ's death (is it really true that we were redeemed by the death of Jesus?);

b)   the bodily resurrection of Jesus (did Christ actually rise from the dead or is it a symbolic account?);

c)   eternal life (is it anything more than wishful thinking to believe that our lives will continue after death?)'

c)   the real presence of Christ in the Eucharist (is this doctrine to be taken literally or is it simply a poetic way of saying that the bread and wine can be a reminder of the Last Supper?);

e)   the Divinity of Christ (instead of saying that Christ is God, is it not sufficient for a Christian to say that Christ is a man whose life is an inspiration for us today—similar to the way that Lincoln can be an inspiration for Americans today?).

As might be imagined, the Vatican was deeply disturbed at this attack on some of the most basic beliefs of Catholicism. When Rome attempted to express its concern, however, other "Catholic scholars" rushed to the defense of the "theologian." Oh, some of them took pains to point out that they might personally disagree with certain of their colleague's conclusions. However, they quickly added, this was not the important thing. No, the important thing was to prevent a "Vatican inquisition" and to defend the "right to dissent" at all costs.

Reading about the controversy, one could easily receive the impression that the views advocated by the dissenter were something new, related in some way or other to advances in modern scholarship. In reality, every one of the doctrines called into question by the "Catholic theologian" had been criticized hundreds of years ago—even thousands of years ago—by people who attacked the Catholic Church from without. In some cases, the "new thinking" of the "Catholic theologian" represented the work of 16th century Protestants who were hostile to the Catholic Church. In other cases (as in the questioning of eternal life) the "new thinking" was closer to the work of the atheists and agnostics of past ages. In all cases, however, the one thing that could definitely be said was that the thinking was hundreds of years old. Instead of being advertised as the "latest reflections of Catholic scholars," it would have been more accurate to describe such thinking as "a re-cycling of the views of 16th century sceptics."

While the current attack by "Catholic dissenters" on Church teaching is basically the same as the past attack by non-Catholics, it is considerably more painful. A betrayal from within your own family hurts more than the fiercest onslaught from without. In addition, when the attack comes from outside, it is much easier to set up defenses to shield yourself. Until recently, Catholic schools and newspapers could be relied upon for this purpose. Today, as the cardinals and archbishops have indicated, these very institutions have often fallen into the hands of the dissenters. Instead of being instruments of defense, they are now instruments of attack. Instead of building up, they now destroy.

According to Archbishop Sheen, a lack of holiness is the cause of this internal attack. It would be easy to apply the Archbishop's statement only to the dissenters. After all, the revolt thay have launched is based upon the pride that the dissenters have in their own brilliance. They are firmly convinced that they know so much that they can decide for themselves which Church teachings to accept and which to reject. How dare the Church judge them! They will judge the Church. How dare the Pope attempt to tell them what to do! They will tell the Pope what to do.

Such an attitude reveals a spirit that is puffed up with pride, the most dangerous of all sins. Nevertheless, we who wish to defend the Church's teaching would ourselves be guilty of pride if we assumed that only the other people were at fault. In fact, we must be careful never to claim that we are holier than the dissenters. That is a judgment to be left to God alone. Our goal is to promote the Church's teaching, not our own personal superiority.

In the Bible, God often gives a warning to the people He has chosen for a particular mission. The warning is a simple one. Do not presume that you have been chosen for your own abilities. Do not presume that you are holier or superior in other ways to the people to whom you are sent. To the contrary, God frequently chooses to work through the weak things of this world in order to confound the strong.

While always being conscious of our own weakness, we must try as hard as we can to advance in God's grace. To defend the Pope and promote the teaching of Christ is a spiritual mission. As Archbishop Sheen indicates, we will only be successful in this mission to the extent that we have become holy. Only then will Our Lord be able to work through us in the way that He wants.

NOTES

[1] Quotation 1 (Cardinal Seper) can be found in the May 4, 1972 edition of

Origins, the documentary periodical of the National Catholic News Service.

[2] Quotation 2 is from Cardinal Wright's Preface (p. 13) to *The Teaching of Christ: A Catholic Catechism for Adults* by Ronald Lawler, Donald Wuerl, and Thomas Lawler (Huntington, Indiana, Our Sunday Visitor, Inc., 1976).

Quotation 3 (Archbishop Laghi) is from a letter sent by the Apostolic Delegate to the bishops of the United States in April 1981.

Quotation 4 (Archbishop Sheen) can be found on page 98 of *The Crisis of Authority: John Paul II and the American Bishops* by Msgr. George A. Kelly (Chicago, Ill., Regnery Gateway Company, 1982).

Quotation 5 (Archbishop Sheen) is from a cassette tape by Bishop Sheen—"A Tribute to a Pope—The Heart of Paul VI" (Pomfret, Maryland, Ministr-O-Media, Inc., 1978).

2.
The Effect of Dissent
on Younger Catholics

What effect have the dissenters had on younger Catholics, that is, on those Catholics who have been learning their religion in Catholic schools (especially high schools and colleges) during the last few years? Why have the dissenters had this effect?

What effect have the dissenters had on loyal Catholics, whether young or old, who continue to believe strongly in the Pope and traditional Catholic teaching? Why have the dissenters had this effect?

These two sets of questions will be the subject of the next three chapters. In this chapter, we will consider the younger Catholics. How has the climate of dissent affected their religious belief and practice? To answer this question, let us take the unusual step of quoting three prominent dissenters themselves. Because I wish to discuss their ideas rather than attack them personally, I will not name the individuals involved. Nevertheless, I wish to assure the reader that the dissenters are being quoted accurately.

Our first witness is a priest who regularly ridicules the Pope and Catholic doctrine. Like most dissenters, however, he used to believe strongly in everything the Church taught. He himself says that when he was first ordained, "I followed all the rules." Now, of course, he considers himself above all that.

During his loyal period, this dissenter undertook an extensive sociological study of Catholic schools. Because he was studying the Catholic educational system prior to the rise of dissent, his report is a good reminder of the effect that Catholic schools once had. What the dissenter found was that the pre-Vatican II Catholic schools were remarkably successful in promoting

Catholic doctrine. To be specific, his research revealed that the students who attended Catholic schools were likely to have the following beliefs and practices as a result:

a)   regular attendance at Sunday Mass;
b)   reception of Holy Communion at least monthly;
c)   confession at least several times a year;
d)   Catholic education of their own children;
e)   acceptance of the Church as an authoritative teacher on faith and morals;
f)   acknowledgment and support of the authority of the Pope and the bishops;
g)   acceptance of the Church's teaching in all areas of sexual morality, even when the following of that teaching involved personal sacrifice
h)   a more detailed knowledge of their religion than that possessed by Catholics who did not attend these schools;
i)   informality with the clergy.

That was the effect of pre-Vatican II Catholic schools. But what about the post-Vatican schools?

Fifteen years after the Council, a close associate of the priest-dissenter conducted another study. The results?

a)   80% of young Catholics reject the teaching of the Church on sexual matters;
b)   almost as many reject the infallibility of the Pope;
c)   only 37% of the young attend Mass weekly;
d)   Catholic education itself is no guarantee of full acceptance by its students of Catholic doctrine.

As one prominent educator remarked in looking at the post-Vatican report: "This represents an almost complete reversal of young Catholic behavioral response in a single generation."

Of course, whenever we are considering polls taken by Church dissenters, we must be careful not to accept the results uncritically. Polls by Church dissenters have a remarkable tendency to prove whatever the dissenters want them to prove. In this case, however, the findings of the dissenter's survey seem to be supported both by other polls and by the personal observations of many loyal Catholics.

As one example, the American bishops themselves sponsored a poll on abortion. This poll produced both good and bad news. On the bad side, the survey found that more than 80% of American Catholics disagreed with the Church's moral position on abortion to some extent—a finding that tends to confirm the results of the dissenter's poll. On the good side, the survey commissioned by the bishops revealed that the situation was definitely not a hopeless one. Catholics were willing to listen to the bishops on abortion and regarded the voice of the Church as an important one. The problem was that they were also being influenced by other voices—voices that had a very different position on abortion from the bishops. (For instance, the bishops' poll concluded that while Catholics considered the Church to be an important source of their information on abortion, they regarded their daily newspaper and television as even more important sources. This created a serious problem for the bishops since, as an ABC television executive once admitted publicly, the press and television tend to report the news in a way sympathetic to the pro-abortion position.)

In summary, the bishops were in a competition. They were not doomed to lose, but they would have to work very hard to win. At stake was the conscience of the Catholic community and the survey was giving the bishops a message that could be paraphrased as follows: It all depends upon whether you are more effective in communicating your values than the other side is in communicating theirs. If your teaching is to have any real impact on Catholics, a simple statement is not enough—no matter how fine that statement may be. To succeed, you must develop pro-life programs in your parishes and schools that strongly reinforce your verbal teaching on abortion. Like everyone else, Catholics are influenced by those around them and it is usually through their local parish or school that they come into contact with the Church. If there is a strong pro-life atmosphere in their local parishes, then your message on abortion will be communicated to the 'grass-roots' Catholic. If there is little or no pro-life activity on the local Catholic level, then the Catholic laity will listen to those other voices and their position on abortion will differ very little from that of their non-Catholic neighbors.

Later in this book, we will suggest that what the bishops' survey revealed about abortion is also true with respect to Church doctrine in general. The official Church teaching is in a competition with other voices that are seeking to win the allegiance of the Catholic laity. The Church can win this competition, but only if her official teaching is strongly supported by effective activity at the local level. To provide such support was once the function of Catholic schools and religious education programs—and it is still their function in theory. In practice, however, these local programs are often controlled by Church dissenters with the predictable result that it is their challenge to the Pope and not the Church's teaching that is reinforced.

To return to the polls, however, there have been a number of other surveys that have produced results similar to the two polls we have already cited. Nor is the problem confined to the United States. In Holland, where dissent has been strong in recent years, a poll revealed that only forty-seven percent of Dutch Catholics believe that Christ is the Son of God. Even fewer Dutch Catholics believe in life after death. As in the United States, the Dutch results represent a widespread abandonment of traditional Catholic beliefs since the Second Vatican Council.

As I write these words, I have just read a religious newspaper that contains a remarkable statement by yet a third prominent Church dissenter. Six months ago, this priest-dissenter was featured on a national television show as a leading American opponent of the Pope's teaching. He was well deserving of the "honor" because he has lashed out repeatedly at the official Catholic teaching in many key areas.

Without in any way modifying his own personal attacks upon the Pope and Catholic doctrine, the priest-dissenter now admits that he faces a serious problem. As the head of the theology department at one of the most important Catholic universities in the country, he has discovered two things that disturb him. First, the Catholic tradition at his college is in danger of disappearing. Second, the students at his Catholic university are learning almost nothing about their religion. To quote this priest-dissenter directly:

> I have been criticized from the left for trying to make this a Catholic department, to recover the Catholic tradition here . . . one of the strengths of the old theology was that it also communicated a lot of information. Even if you came away liberal, you at least knew a lot of information. Now these people don't have *any* information. Whether liberal or conservative, they don't know what the Catholic past has been.

As we study the picture presented in the last few pages, a number of things become apparent:

1) The revolt is not simply against one or two Church teachings. It involves virtually every Catholic doctrine, including the most important beliefs of our religion.

2) There are serious differences among the dissenters themselves. The only bond that unites them is their challenge to the Pope.

3) As might be expected, many Catholic students no longer believe in those Church teachings that have been openly ridiculed by the

dissenters. As might not be expected, however, the loss of faith extends also to doctrines the dissenters have not rejected publicly and it even extends to beliefs that the dissenters would like their students to keep.

The Extent of the Crisis

The secular press and television have often highlighted the activity of the dissenters on issues such as contraception and the ordaining of women to the priesthood. For that reason, it is sometimes assumed that only two or three Church teachings are under attack. In reality, the crisis involves virtually every belief of the Catholic religion including the divinity of Jesus, the Real Presence of Our Lord in the Eucharist, the reality of eternal life, and the Resurrection. Is it just a few "far out" theologians who deny these truths? As additional evidence that this is not the case, let us quote both a Cardinal and a Pope.[2]

Cardinal William Baum of Washington was chosen by Pope John Paul II to head the Sacred Congregation for Catholic Education, the Vatican department that oversees Catholic education and seminaries. Prior to this appointment, Cardinal Baum served as the head of the American Bishops' Doctrinal Committee. Speaking of the Incarnation, the belief that Jesus is both God and man, Cardinal Baum reported to the American Bishops that this central truth of our faith is now under widespread attack from theological dissenters. As the Cardinal put it:

> The mystery of the Incarnation is being challenged in a profound new way by many theologians and if you have not felt the effects of this in your own local dioceses, you will in time. These effects already are being felt in our seminaries and universities, and undoubtedly will affect preaching and teaching in the local churches.

Cardinal Baum went on to add that many of the attacks were similar to heresies condemned by the Church in the fourth and fifth centuries. In other words, the much heralded "new thinking" is nothing but the "old heresy" and represents no advance in scholarship at all.

The Cardinal also tells us where the attack is coming from. It originates in the academic world, with those who consider themselves to be the intellectual elite. From there the dissent eventually seeps down to the parish level, although a period of time may pass before this happens.

Pope John Paul I made a similar comment in 1978. A few weeks before he was elected Pope, the then Cardinal Luciani wrote an article about the attack on Catholic beliefs. Using the parish sermon as an example, he expressed concern that today's preaching "never speaks of the following tragedies of original sin, purgatory, hell, the last judgment." Cardinal Luciani continues: "Rare are the preachers who speak to the young about continence and self-control. Often the preachers let it be believed, explicitly or implicitly, that such points of Catholic doctrine, taught until recently, are false, superficial, or dépassé."

To illustrate the problem, the future Pope presented the example of sermons that took place in a large church in Italy. One week, a theologian denied the humanity of Jesus. The next week, another theologian denied the divinity of Jesus. A few weeks later, a third preacher cast doubt on the historical existence of Jesus!

Dissent Among the Dissenters

It is easy to think of the dissenters as one solid group besieging the Pope. In reality, there are many groups among the dissenters and these groups are sometimes quite hostile to each other. They agree on challenging the authority of the Holy Father, but they disagree on everything else.

How much authority should be stripped from the Papacy, all of it or only a part? If only a part, which part? Who should get the authority that they intend to take from the Pope? How many Church beliefs should be thrown out, a few or a great many? What should be put in their place? Which doctrines, if any, should definitely be retained?

No matter how revolutionary a dissenter may be, there is usually another dissenter around who is even more revolutionary. Amazingly (in view of their own attacks upon the Pope), the less revolutionary dissenters will then accuse the others of being "disloyal to the Catholic tradition." What they are really saying is this: "You aren't allowed to throw out any doctrines except those which we and our friends have decided to discard." Needless to say, the more revolutionary dissenters are not too impressed by that argument.

A second practice of the "less revolutionary" dissenters is to use the position of their radical colleagues as a public relations device to "prove" that they themselves are "moderate" and "balanced."

"You see," they will tell you, "there are two extremes. On one extreme are the conservatives, the fundamentalists, the right-wingers. These are the people who believe in *all* the teachings of the Church. On the other extreme are the leftwingers, the radicals. These are the people who believe in *none* of the teachings of the Church. Both these groups are extremist. In between, however, are the people who are not extremists—those who are mature and balanced and capable of thinking for themselves. These are the Catholics who accept some of the teachings of the Church but reject others. They are the Catholics who are intelligent and open-minded. They are, in short, the Catholics who agree with us."

To appreciate the trick that is being played here, suppose that you came upon a gentleman who is an arsonist. He has the nice little habit of burning down buildings. However, he is very careful not to start a fire unless the building is unoccupied.

"You see," he explains to you, "there are two extremes. On one extreme are the conservatives, the fundamentalists, the right-wingers. These are the people who believe you should not burn down buildings at all. On the other extreme are the left-wingers, the radicals. These are the people who believe you should burn down buildings whenever you want, even if they are occupied. In between are the people who are moderates. They reject the rigid and inflexible rule that says one should not set fire to buildings but they also reject the 'do whatever you want' attitude. Because this position avoids the extremism of both the right and left, it is a responsible position, a balanced position. Its advocates have shown an impressive ability to think things through for themselves and to combine in an open and flexible way the best elements of the radicals and the conservatives while rejecting the unfortunate excesses of both groups."

Such rhetoric illustrates two tactics frequently employed by Church dissenters to boost their own position while discrediting anybody who disagrees with them. The first tactic is to claim the middle. "Claiming the middle" is something it is almost always possible to do. For example, if I am seven feet in height, most people would consider me very tall indeed. Nevertheless, people do exist who are taller. If for some reason I want to "claim the middle," I simply point to a person who stands seven feet, two inches. Then I suggest that anybody who is above seven feet is "on one extreme" and anybody who is below seven feet is "on the other extreme." Thus, by a curious coincidence, the "middle" becmes seven feet—the exact place at which I happen to be.

The second tactic of the dissenters is to use warm and sympathetic words to describe their own opinion—words such as "moderate," "balanced," "open-minded," "responsible," "creative," "modern." At the same time, cold and harsh-sounding words are used to describe the views of Catholics who adhere to Church teaching—"rigid," "inflexible," "fundamentalist," "right-wing," "extremist," "old-fashioned," "unthinking," "narrow."

This is the "labelling" tactic of the dissenters. What they are really doing by such labelling is engaging in a form of advertising. Certain modern advertisers have deliberately rejected the idea that the way to sell a product is to talk about its merits. Instead of discussing what their product can actually do, these advertisers believe that the best sales approach is to associate their product emotionally with a quality that their customers are presumed to want. Thus, an automobile manufacturer who believes in this form of advertising will put commercials on television that say little or nothing about the actual merits of the car. For example, there will be no discussion about how many miles per gallon of gas a customer can expect from the car. That would involve selling the car on its merits. Instead, the television commercials will show beautiful young women and handsome young men—all of them happy and all of them admiring the car. As the advertisers themselves admit frankly, the theory is that automobiles can be sold by associating them with qualities that people want, namely, youth and beauty and happiness. "If you buy our car, you will be irresistible to the opposite sex." Logically, such a message is nonsense, but psychologically, if sales research is to be believed, it is not. Advertisers are prepared to spend millions of dollars on such an approach because they are convinced that sales will jump substantially if such an emotional identification can be made.

The "sales approach" of many Church dissenters is similar. They don't sell dissent to the public by means of a logical approach. They don't sell dissent by a reasoned discussion of the merits of their position, and they certainly don't sell dissent by a discussion of the merits of the Church position they are rejecting. Like the automobile advertiser, they sell dissent to the public by an emotional process that has nothing to do with the actual worth of their product—a process that involves the repeated identification of their position with qualities that people want ("moderation," "openness," "balance," etc.) and the repeated identification of the Church's position with qualities that people despise ("rigidity," "narrowness," "obsolescense," etc.).

In line with this sales approach, most Church dissenters are reluctant to engage in any sort of debate with defenders of the Pope's teaching, especially if the defender of the Holy Father is knowledgeable and articulate. The reluctance of the dissenters exists even where the "debate" would take place in an atmosphere that is calm and free of hostility. In fact, it might well be said that Church dissenters are especially reluctant to "debate" under such circumstances. Why? Because in a situation that is relatively calm, there is an excellent chance that the audience will begin to concentrate its attention on what the defender of the Pope is actually saying. Once this happens it will be increasingly difficult for the dissenters to caricature the traditional Catholic position and to dismiss the Pope's view by branding it with a host of unsympathetic adjectives. Instead of encouraging such an exchange, therefore, a major strategy of the dissenters is to keep the Catholic public from hearing any effective presentation of the traditional Church teaching.

Note that this attitude of the dissenters involves an important admission—the admission that the defenders of the Pope would at least hold their own in any fair exchange. If the dissenters were convinced that they could demonstrate their intellectual superiority in such debates, they would rush to have them because there is no more effective way to win popular support than to beat your oponent in a discussion that takes place before the public's very eyes. Instead of pursuing such a strategy, the dissenters lean over backwards to avoid it.

From the dissenter's point of view, such a decision is understandable. They have been selling dissent by the emotional "labelling" technique described above. Furthermore, they have worked hard to promote the line that people with intelligence must reject the Church's taching and accept their view. Both these maneuvers could be thoroughly discredited by any discussion that concentrated on the merits.

Loss of Faith Beyond the Dissenters

To this point we have discussed the wide extent of the present crisis of faith and commented on the fact that the dissenters often dissent among themselves. In addition, we have looked at three public-relations tactics of the dissenters ("claiming the middle," "labelling," avoiding any discussions that would give defenders of the Pope an opportunity to present their case effectively). Let us now examine the important difference between what the dissenters intend and what they actually accomplish.

According to the poll of the Church dissenters that we cited previously, the young Catholics who have been exposed to dissent have the following attitudes:

a) 80% reject the teaching of the Chuch on sexual matters;
b) almost as many reject the infallibility of the Pope;
c) only 37% of the young attend Mass weekly;

The Church's teaching on sexual morality, the belief in Papal infallibility, regular attendance at Mass: all of them are rejected by the vast majority of young Catholics. Yet, if we think about it, the dissenters themselves take a very different public position with respect to each of these three questions.

In regard to the Church's teaching on sexual morality, the dissenters were loud and vocal in their opposition, particularly on the question of contraception. On the infallibility of the Pope, however, most dissenters (at least in the early years after Vatican II) insisted they believed in the doctrine. As outlined in our previous book, *Defending the Papacy*, the dissenters usually "justified" their opposition to the Pope on contraception by the following argument: We certainly accept the fact that teachings of the extraordinary magisterium are infallible, and we would never think of denying Papal infallibility in these areas. However, since the Church's teaching on contraception involves the ordinary magisterium, we do not believe it falls into this category. Despite the repeated protestations of the dissenters that they would never deny infallibility, young Catholics now reject this doctrine to almost the same extent that they reject the Holy Father's teaching on sexual morality.

On regular Mass attendance, there has also been a sharp decline among young Catholics exposed to dissent. Yet it would be hard to find a dissenter who would do anything but deplore such a trend. While many dissenters believe there should be no Church requirement to attend Mass, and while they have often made unauthorized changes in the Masses they celebrate, they usually say that the Mass itself is important and they urge their followers to attend regularly. Nevertheless, if their own polls are to be believed, most young Catholics have reached a very different conclusion.

What we have, therefore, are three different attitudes among the dissenters themselves, *but the same result among the young Catholics exposed to dissent*. Whether the Church teaching is one that the dissenters publicly reject (as with contraception), or whether it is one that the dissenters do not stress but support with lip-service (as with the infallibility of the Pope), or whether it is one that the dissenters support in a public and active way (as with frequent Mass attendance), the same negative result occurs among the majority of young Catholics. Whether the Church taching is attacked, ignored, or supported by the dissenters, it is abandoned by most young Catholics exposed to the climate of dissent. They lose their faith even in those beliefs that their dissenter-teachers would like them to retain.

Why does such a sharp difference exist between the intentions of the dissenters and the effect that their dissent has on Catholics exposed to it? To understand what appears to be happening, an example might be helpful. Recently there was a court case in which a man was accused of killing his wife. A key question considered at the trial was whether the husband was sane or insane at the moment of the crime. The lawyer prosecuting the man argued that he was sane at the time of the act. In support of his claim, the prosecution attorney put five psychiatrists on the witness stand. As experts on the matter, they all testified that the husband was definitely sane.

When the time came for the defense to present its case, the lawyer for the accused husband put five other psychiatrists on the witness stand. These psychiatrists promptly contradicted everything that the other psychiatrists had said. With the same air of self-confidence that the experts on the other side had previously exhibited, the defense psychiatrists assured the jury that the husband was definitely insane.

What was the effect of such contradictory testimony? According to newspaper accounts, the result was that the jury lost all faith in the "expert" statements. A juror interviewed after the trial was over reported that he and his colleagues found the psychiatric testimony so mixed up that they decided to disregard it altogether and decide the case on other grounds.

In the same way, the Church dissenters want young Catholics to regard their own expertise highly. It is only the authority of traditional Church teachings that they wish to discredit. Nevertheless, their "theological dissent" caused most young Catholics to be sceptical of almost everything. Like the jury faced with ten psychiatrists, young Catholics conclude that things are so mixed up that it would be foolish to believe anybody.

What we have described above is something that frequently happens to those who start revolutions—and it was a revolution the dissenters launched when they challenged Church teachings in the years after Vatican II. Such revolutionaries are often unable to control the events they have set into motion. What they intend is a simple maneuver. They want to replace the existing authority with themselves. What they achieve is something quite different—a state of anarchy, the collapse of all authority. Like a runaway roller-coaster, the revolution they began is now totally out of control.

They taught others to reject authority. Now they wring their hands and complain: "But we never meant for them to reject us too."

Conclusion: The Three Groups

We have been considering the effects of Church dissent upon young Catholics. In doing so, we have been careful to use the phrase "most young Catholics." Like every other group, Catholics exposed to dissent can react in different ways. In fact, if we look closely, we see that there are really three different groups of young Catholics.

First, there is a group of young Catholics who have remained faithful to the Pope and traditional Church teaching. Even the dissenters themselves admit that 15% to 20% of young Catholics would belong to this category. With these Catholics, the dissenters have failed in their goal of undermining the authority of the Holy Father. It is a remarkable achievement that these young men and women have remained faithful in such trying circumstances.

Second, there is a group of young Catholics who accept the Church dissenters as their leaders. With this group, the dissenters have succeeded totally. Where the American Catholic Church goes in the future will be determined largely by the struggle between this group and the first group that is loyal to the Pope.

In the contest between these two groups, the Catholics loyal to the Pope have one surprising advantage. The advantage of Catholics loyal to the Pope is that they appear at present to have the greater numbers. If this conclusion sounds surprising, please remember that we are comparing the Catholics loyal to the Pope with the Catholics loyal to the dissenters. We are not considering the third group of Catholics who do not accept either the authority of the Pope or the authority of the dissenters.

Among those Catholics who have rejected the authority of the Pope, the great majority as we have seen have no particular loyalty to the beliefs of the dissenters. In fact, the majority probably do not even know the names of the principal Church dissenters. They have certainly been affected by the climate of scepticism created by the dissenters but this does not mean that they are "fans" who enthusiastically follow the dissenters.

For public relations purposes, the dissenters usually do not emphasize the difference between such Catholics and the group of Catholics who are loyal to them. Since the dissenters want people to believe that they have overwhelming numbers on their side, their works frequently suggest that there are only two groups of Catholics—those loyal to the Pope's teaching and those loyal to the dissenters. With glee they point out that "only 20%" of young Catholics accept the Pope's teaching, thus creating the impression that the other 80% follow the dissenters. (Having created this impression, they then suggest further to Church authorities that if only the Church were to abandon its traditional teaching and adopt the views of the dissenters then the 80% who are "loyal" to the dissenters would return to the fold and become practicing Catholics once more.)

In reality, the true situation appears closer to the following:

a) 15% to 20% are firmly loyal to the Pope (Group I);
b) 5% are firmly loyal to the dissenters (Group II);
c) 75% to 80% have been so affected by the climate of confusion

that they are not sure what, if anything, they believe and they cannot be listed presently as supporting either the authority of the Pope or the authority of the dissenters (Group III).

Admittedly, such figures are approximate. They could also change substantially in the future. For now, however, I believe it can safely be said that Group III is by far the largest group, but that Group I (Catholics with a firm loyalty to the Pope) remains considerably larger than Group II (Catholics with a firm loyalty to the dissenters).

The significance of these numbers becomes apparent when we realize that what happens in the future will be determined by those people who work actively for their beliefs—not by those who remain passive. Precisely because the climate of dissent has caused them to become confused and even sceptical, the young Catholics in Group III are unlikely to become activists either for the Pope or for the dissenters. The struggle for the future will be fought between Group I and Group II.

While the group of Catholics that is loyal to the Pope presently has the greater numbers, the group that is devoted to the dissenters presently has a higher percentage of Church activists. A major goal of those Catholics who wish to support the Holy Father must be to reach out to their "constituency," that is, to the millions of Catholics who agree with them—and to activate this constituency on behalf of the traditional Catholic teachings that are being attacked by the dissenters. It is not a lack of concern that keeps many loyal Catholics from becoming active, but an uncertainty about what they can do or a belief that their activity is not needed since somebody else is taking care of the problem.

A final comment with reference to the large third group we have described throughout this chapter, the young Catholics who have become increasingly sceptical of both traditional Church teachings and the claims of the dissenters. This group of young Catholics are the tragic victims of the current climate of dissent. While the "Catholic theologians" who attack the Pope righteously deny any responsibility for the loss of faith on the part of these young Catholics, the truth is otherwise. How sad that, as Bishop Sheen stated, it has been Catholic schools themselves that have often been a source of scandal to young Catholics and led them to abandon their faith. Those who scandalized the young by their ridicule of the Holy Father might do well to recall the words of Jesus in the 18th chapter of St. Matthew's Gospel:

But whoever causes one of these little ones who believe in me to sin, it were better for him to have a great millstone hung around his neck, and to be drowned in the depths of the sea. Woe to the world because of scandals! For it must needs be that scandals come, but woe to the man through whom scandal does come!

NOTES

[1] For example, a similar Dutch poll was taken in 1966. This survey came at a time when dissent had been rampant in Holland for several years but had not yet become as firmly entrenched as it would later. As a result, the 1966 poll showed 70% of Dutch Catholics believed that Christ was God. The fact that only 70% believed in this most important of Catholic truths demonstrates the effect dissent was already having. The subsequent sharp drop from 70% to 45% illustrates that dissent, if not effectively checked, will grow stronger as the years pass and will be increasingly successful in eroding the Catholic faith.

[2] These two quotations may be found on pages 13 and 14 of *A Crisis of Truth: The Attack on Faith, Morality, and Mission in the Catholic Church* by Ralph Martin (Servant Books: Ann Arbor, Mich.)

3.
The Effect of Dissent on Loyal Catholics

This chapter will consider the impact of dissent on loyal Catholics. Since the previous chapter studied the effect of dissent on the faith of young Catholics, I should emphasize at the outset that I have no intention of suggesting either that young Catholics are not loyal or that loyal Catholics are all elderly.

The distinction I have in mind is the following. When considering "young Catholics," I was writing about those young men and women who were receiving (or are receiving) their religious formation in "Catholic" schools or programs influenced by the dissenters. Usually these men and women are relatively young in age. Even if they are not, however, they are "young Catholics" in the sense that they are just in the process of receiving their training in Catholic teachings. Instead of strengthening these Catholics in their faith, the "Catholic" schools influenced by the dissenters often put obstacles in their paths and make it very difficult for them to believe.

In writing about "loyal Catholics," on the other hand, I am considering men and women who (whatever their age) have already made a firm commitment to the Holy Father and to Catholic teaching. Although it is always possible to deepen one's knowledge of Catholicism, these Catholics have received their basic religious formation. Often they were fortunate to attend Catholic schools that were really Catholic—schools free from the influence of the dissenters. If not, they somehow managed to overcome the climate of dissent around them. They are now committed deeply to the Church's official teaching, including those doctrines that the dissenters ridicule.

In looking at the effect of dissent on these loyal Catholics, it must first be pointed out that people can react to the same situation in very different ways. We saw this with respect to "young Catholics" in the last chapter, and it is equally true of "loyal Catholics."

Some loyal Catholics are suffering terribly because of dissent. Others are not. If these two classes of loyal Catholics are to work together in support of the Pope, they must be sensitive to each other's feelings. That is the purpose of this chapter, to help loyal Catholics with similar convictions but different feelings to communicate with each other. Let us begin with the Catholics who are suffering very much.

Priests Loyal to the Pope

In December 1981, the *Homiletic and Pastoral Review* published an unusual article entitled "The Plight of the Papist Priest." Its author was identified only as "A Parish Priest." As the editor commented in an explanatory note: "The 'Parish Priest' who wrote this article wishes to remain anonymous for obvious reasons. Normally, we do not print unsigned material, but we have made a few exceptions. This is one of them. The author gives strong expression to the painful dilemma many priests now find themselves in."

The reaction to the article in the months that followed confirmed the editor's view that the writer was expressing the feelings of many priests who are loyal to the Pope but who feel isolated in their dioceses or religious communities. Moreover, the article stimulated a rash of similar letters from deacons and lay people. Since the situation described by these "papist" Catholics is likely to continue for many years (even many decades) after 1981, let us look closely at what they are saying to us.

The "Papist priests" feel lonely and powerless. In a moment we will look at these feelings more closely. Let us begin, however, by summarizing in four points the problem as those priests see it.

1) Catholic schools, newspapers, and other Church institutions are influenced to a great extent by the dissenters and often promote their views at the expense of the Pope's teaching.

2) The bishop does nothing about it. In fact, in some cases the bishop appears to favor what is happening.

3) Attendance at education programs dominated by the dissenters is sometimes made mandatory by the bishop. Meanwhile, orthodox catechisms are banned from the diocese and speakers favorable to the Pope's position

are not invited.

4) Priests who speak out against these abuses are punished.

Sadly, the four points listed above are indeed a true description of what is happening in many places. Point One (about Catholic schools, newspapers, religious education programs, etc.) is similar to the comments we have already seen from Cardinal Wright, Archbishop Laghi, and Archbishop Sheen. Point Two corresponds to Cardinal Seper's statement, although the Cardinal did not go so far as to say that some bishops actually favored the dissenters.

Points Three and Four can also be documented by many specific examples. What these points reflect is the fact that priests and religious sympathetic to the dissenters often occupy key administrative posts within a parish or diocese, especially in areas related to religious education. As a result, they are in a position to determine the make-up of official Church programs. They decide what columns to run in the diocesan newspaper and what columns not to run, what speakers to invite to a meeting of all the clergy and what speakers not to invite, what books to approve for the Catholic schools and what books not to approve. Often they choose the works of Church dissenters while rejecting the works of Catholics who support the Pope's teaching.

As for Point Four, the dissenters have made it clear that they will make things as difficult as possible for anybody who gets in their way. If they treat the Pope himself with such ridicule, can they be expected to be any less vicious when the obstacle in their path is a parish priest or a layman, or, for that matter, a bishop? Therefore, if priests who support the dissenters are on the diocesan personnel board and can influence assignments, they may well do whatever is in their power to keep priests who openly support the Pope out of key positions in the diocese. They will argue that such "papist" priests are controversial, that they have closed minds, that they are not up-to-date theologically. The message of dissenters to other Catholics is a simple one: "If you keep silent, if you do not challenge us, if you allow us to do whatever we wish, then you will have no problems. On the other hand, if you stand up to us, if you create difficulties, then you in turn will be hit so hard that you will be very sorry you ever opened your mouths."

Faced with these tactics, priests loyal to the Holy Father have a choice to make. In the words of one of the priests who wrote to the *Homiletic and Pastoral Review*: "More and more of those who have similarly agonized seem to be deserting into early retirement or 'to get along you gotta go along' . . . "

However, it is not simply fear of the consequences that causes many priests to remain silent. There is also a problem of conscience. The author of the article describes the conscience problem this way:

> The basic question is what do we papist priests do when we experience a conflict between the authority of the Holy Father and the authority of our local bishop? What are we to do when the bishop, directly or indirectly through his officials, orders us to disregard (and in fact disobey) repeated and insistent papal directives? Do we obey the bishop or the pope? To state the question seems to answer it, but to know the answer in theory is not to solve it in practice . . . The questions become specific: Must we attend lectures given by heretics when the bishop so insists? Should we feel justified in concelebrating with priests who openly deny essentials of the faith including the doctrine of the Real Presence, or when glaring abuses take place and we seem to endorse them by our participation? What should be our stance in regard to the people committed to our pastoral care? Must we remain silent forever about the errors and abuses which inundate them? Dare we risk causing scandal by warning our faithful people about this spiritual poison when they know that specific priests and perhaps the bishop himself are prescribing it? We have been prudential for years; is this a virtue or a vice?

The author is saying that many loyal priests choose to be silent rather than to speak out concerning the errors and abuses around them. Why? Not simply because of the personal danger involved in challenging the dissenters. No, there is a more important reason. Many loyal priests sincerely believe that if they did speak out that would make the situation even worse. "Dare we risk causing scandal by warning our faithful people about this spiritual poison when they know that specific priests and perhaps the bishop himself are prescribing it?" If the priests supporting the official Church teachings go public and reveal what is happening, many Catholics might be disillusioned. Perhaps some would even leave the faith as a result. Are there not times when a lack of knowledge can actually protect people? If the loyal priests remain silent, their parishioners may never realize the full extent of what is going on, and this could keep them from being "scandalized."

On the other hand, silence could work in exactly the opposite way. Instead of protecting the faithful from scandal, it could leave their parishioners unprepared to face the attacks of the dissenters upon Church doctrine. Perhaps it is an illusion to believe that the laity do not know what is taking place. Suppose they understand only too well and are confused or frustrated as a result. What happens then if the priests remain silent? Will such silence deprive many loyal Catholics of the strong support they need to remain faithful? Could such silence even be interpreted as a kind of acceptance of the present situation in which dissent to the Pope is promoted so openly? The decision to publicly challenge abuses or to remain silent is a painful one precisely because it is possible to argue both ways—that speaking out will make things even worse for the faithful or that speaking out is absolutely necessary to support the faith of loyal Catholics. As the author of the article describes this dilemma: "We have been prudent for years; is this a virtue or a vice?"

Are the Bishops in the Same Quandry?

One reason I have outlined in some detail this dilemma of the "papist" priests is to suggest that many bishops may be in the same situation. If there is one point that comes through clearly in the writings of the loyal priests, it is their total frustration at the silence of the bishops. In some cases, the bishop assures the loyal priests privately that he agrees with them. Publicly, however, no effort is made to check the influence of the dissenters who continue to dominate the diocesan programs.

For example, one of the priests who wrote to the *Homiletic and Pastoral Review* tells the story of a mandatory retreat that was held for all the priests of his diocese. The retreat master used the occasion to propagandize for the view that dissent from the teaching of the Holy Father is proper and legitimate. Privately, the bishop expressed his strong disagreement with the retreat master. Yet the bishop said nothing in public and it was the bishop who provided the dissenter with a captive audience by ordering all the priests to come and listen.

This discrepancy between the words of the bishop and what is actually happening at the bishop's official programs comes across as hypocrisy to many of the "papist" priests. As the priest himself puts it: "In any case when objection is made to the person or the programs of Religious Education, CCD, or any of the multitude of bureaucrats spawned in the new system, the bishop declares himself pro-pontiff, demands channels be maintained, and supports those who have the channel gates guarded against orthodoxy . . . So when the bishop talks about papal fidelity the saying goes out— 'Words are cheap.' "

It is understandable that loyal priests feel frustrated when the bishop verbally supports the Holy Father but at the same time sponsors diocesan programs that promote dissent from the Pope's teaching. As the quotations from Cardinal Seper and the Apostolic Delegate make clear, the Vatican shares this frustration. Nevertheless, I do not think that the "papist" priests should assume immediately that such silent bishops do not care. After all, the loyal priests admit that they themselves were silent for many years even though they cared deeply. They were silent because of the fear that to speak out publicly would be to make things much worse. Perhaps the publicly silent bishops have the same fear. If it is really true, as one of the loyal priests estimates, that three-eighths of the clergy in the diocese are active supporters of the dissenters, then any attempt by the bishop to remove the dissenters from diocesan programs might result in an explosion that could rip the diocese apart. Faced with this kind of revolt, even a strongly loyal bishop might decide that the prudent course is to express his personal support of the Pope while avoiding any action against the dissenters that could lead to a public confrontation in the diocese.

To say all this does not mean that the silent bishops have made the correct decision. As we saw earlier with respect to the silence of loyal priests, the silence of loyal bishops can have exactly the opposite effect from what is intended. Instead of making things better, it can make things a hundred times worse. It can give the dissenters the time, the freedom, and the resources they need to turn millions of Catholics away from the Pope's teaching. It allows those who deny important Catholic truths to clothe themselves publicly with the authority of the bishop. No wonder the Vatican is so alarmed by the lack of effective action from many local bishops.

"How You Feel is How They Feel"

In summary, in considering both the bishops above them and the lay people who are their parishioners, the loyal priests might do well to follow this principle: "How you feel will probably be the way that they will feel." If loyal priests sincerely believe that it is more prudent to be silent publicly than to speak out concerning abuses, then they should not be surprised if their bishop reaches a similar conclusion. In the same way, if loyal priests are frustrated and angry at the bishop's silence, then they should expect their loyal parishioners to be equally frustrated and angry at their silence.

Interestingly, one of the letters to the *Homiletic and Pastoral Review* demonstrates this very point. Richard is a layman who feels betrayed by the silence of loyal priests. Accusing such priests of "compromising and dissembling," he writes angrily:

> Thomas More didn't need the Pope to tell him precisely what he wanted him to do! Bishop Fisher wasn't worried about losing his retirement benefits! . . . This is the real tragedy today, that so few clergy are

willing to take a stand, regardless of the consequences. Nothing discourages and confuses the faithful more than to see good priests doing what they know is wrong, out of a false concept of obedience. It is their passive acceptance of the revolution that has enabled it to succeed so well.

Notice that Richard's letter about the "papist" priests mirrors in both tone and content the attitude of the priests toward their bishop. As the priests assume that the public silence of their bishop is caused either by cowardice or a lack of real concern, so Richard assumes that the public silence of "papist" priests is caused either by cowardice or a lack of real concern. As the priests are angered rather than reassured when a publicly silent bishop tells them privately that he is on their side, so Richard is angered rather than reassured by the private comments of publicly quiet priests. As the priests put all the blame for the current situation on the bishops—and insist that only strong action by the bishops (rather than their own action) can solve the problem, so Richard puts the blame on the priests and insists that only activity by the "papist" priests (rather than his own action or the action of other lay people) can correct the situation.

I do not intend to disparage either Richard or the priests. They are expressing what they truly believe—that they are powerless to check dissent themselves and that only somebody with greater authority can act effectively. Nevertheless, I am convinced that such an assumption is the single most important reason that loyal Catholics are far behind the dissenters when it comes to influencing present events within the Church.

Since we will be encountering this attitude throughout the book, let us give it a name and refer to it as "the assumption of powerlessness." People are operating under "the assumption of powerlessness" if what they say can be reduced to the following two sentences:

1. "We ourselves are powerless to change the current state of events."

2. "Only somebody else has this power and they ought to use it."

Having defined the "assumption of powerlessness," let us apply it to dissent within the Church by asking two questions: 1) How many of the loyal Catholics operate under this assumption? 2) How many of the dissenters operate under this assumption?

While I would only be guessing about the exact percentage, I am convinced that an overwhelming majority of faithful Catholics operate under this assumption of powerlessness. In contrast, almost all the dissenters do not. It probably is not exaggerating to say that at least 90% of the dissenters feel that their personal activity can influence events, while at least 90% of the loyal Catholics feel that they themselves are powerless to alter the present climate and that the only route open to them is to ask somebody else (such as the bishop) to act.

The Dissenters Build Their Own "Power Base"

If we look at the activity of the dissenters since the Second Vatican Council, we see that they have grown in influence because of what they themselves have done, not because of what others have done for them. If they had waited for the bishops to endorse dissent, if they had decided that only action by the Church's hierarchy could give them the victory, then they would still be waiting and they would still be powerless.

Instead of relying on others, the dissenters began to act for themselves. They met regularly with other dissenters to plan strategy. Over a period of time, such contacts evolved into a kind of "network" within the Church—a network that would be available to help any Church dissenter whenever trouble arose.

In addition to their meetings with other dissenters, the challengers to the Pope actively sought converts at every opportunity. They worked very, very hard to "sell" dissent to the Catholic community and to increase the numbers of committed dissenters. They wrote books opposing the Church teaching, they gave speeches, they went on lecture tours, they organized rallies and other events designed to get them favorable coverage in the secular newspapers and television, they gave out press releases, they wrote letters to the newspapers, both Catholic and secular, in short, they did everything they could to propagandize for dissent.

All of this was accomplished without any involvement from the bishops. Instead of proclaiming that "only the bishops can do anything effective," the dissenters said, "We can do it ourselves—and we will."

Not that the dissenters have "given up" on the bishops—to the contrary, they hope to obtain eventually the public support of a number of bishops. To bring about a situation in which as many bishops as possible break openly with the Pope over Catholic doctrine is a major long range goal of the dissenters. In pursuit of this goal, those challenging the teaching of the Holy Father neglect no opportunity to meet with bishops (especially the ones considered "sympathetic") in order to "re-educate" them, which means to lobby them on behalf of dissent. In the long run, such efforts could well be successful, especally if Catholics loyal to the Pope are not equally active in meeting bishops and expressing their support for official Church teachings.

If the dissenters do succeed in their "bishop-lobbying," then in the future we will witness a number of bishops issuing a public challenge to the Pope. To the present, however, this has not happened. Instead, the dissenters have achieved great power and influence without any public endorsement of their position by the bishops.

Despite their hopes for public episcopal backing at a later time, the present attitude of the dissenters toward the bishops can be summarized as follows: They don't have to do anything. We'll do it ourselves. All we ask of the bishops is that they stay out of our way. If a bishop interferes with our efforts, if he attempts to remove dissenters from key posts in his diocese or moves in other ways to stop dissent, then we will create an uproar that will rip his diocese to pieces. On the other hand, if the bishop will leave the dissenters alone, then we will take care of the rest.

In contrast to the "do it ourselves" mentality of the dissenters, what is the attitude of those Catholics who are well aware of the dimensions of the crisis and who support the Pope strongly? Almost universally such loyal Catholics operate under the assumption of powerlessness: "There is little or nothing that we ourselves can do. It depends on the action of somebody else."

For example, here is the way that the author of the *Homeletic and Pastoral Review* article expresses the assumption of powerlessness:

> No disorder discussed here can be corrected unless the *bishop* is sound and courageous. Even the seminaries, the crucial next priority, cannot be reconstituted without heroic good shepherds. . . . There is simply no way to reform seminaries, religious education offices, marriage tribunals, the diocese press, liturgical and other abuses, until tough, papally orientated bishops are in position . . . if remedy is not otherwise given by corrective action, the papist priest will have no recourse but to meekly and silently retire. . . ."

Can anyone imagine a dissenter writing that nothing could be accomplished without the personal activity of the bishops and that—if such activity were not forthcoming—then the dissenters would have no recourse but to retire?

There is a saying that the grass is always greener on the other side of the fence. Applying this to the present situation, it can safely be said that many loyal Catholics underestimate their own power to change things for the better while overestimating the power of Catholics in other positions to change things for the better. Thus, if the loyal Catholics are not bishops, they tend to assume that a bishop has great power to check dissent. On the other hand, if the loyal Catholics are bishops, they tend to assume that a bishop has little power to check dissent.

In reality, who is right? Probably neither side. The loyal bishops have more power than they realize but less power than the non-bishops believe. In turn, the non-bishops underestimate their own power to change things as much as the bishops underestimate theirs.

As an illustration of this phenomenon, there is a true story that occurred a few years ago. A group of dissenting American theologians had published a book ridiculing many Church doctrines. Shortly after their work appeared, six loyal Catholics went out for dinner. Three of the Catholics were bishops while the other three were theologians. All of them were deeply disturbed by the action of the dissenters but they disagreed on the best way to counter it.

The three bishops urged the theologians to speak out publicly because the bishops thought that, as experts, the loyal theologians could be very effective in refuting the dissenters. The theologians, in contrast, kept stressing how important it was for Church authority (by which they meant the bishops) to act decisively.

Each side saw something important for the other to do. At the same time, each side felt that they themselves could have little impact. Of course, as long as everybody believes it is someone else who holds the key, nobody will be unlocking the door.

The Right Attitude: I Will Do What I Can

Why do loyal Catholics feel so powerless? Could one reason be that they are concentrating their attention on the things they cannot do instead of looking at the things they can do? The Christopher movement has a motto: "Better to light one candle than to curse the darkness." The darkness is vast and the light from a single candle does not provide much illumination. Nevertheless, it is still of some help. Furthermore, if everybody were to light his or her individual candle, then the effect would be tremendous.

As Edward Everett Hale wrote:

I am only one,
   But still I am one.
I cannot do everything,
   But still I can do something;
And because I cannot do everything
   I will not refuse to do the something that I can do.

Many loyal Catholics are acutely aware that they cannot do everything. They also know that there are other Catholics who are in a position to light a candle that would be far brighter than theirs. Knowing this, they keep hoping and praying that the people with the large candles will make use of their opportunity. Meanwhile, however, they should never forget to light their own candles. Although the opportunities they have to advance Catholic doctrine may be much more limited than those possessed by others, the opportunities are still there. The light from a thousand small candles can be a very bright light indeed.

"Because I cannot do everything, I will not neglect to do the something that I can do." If all the loyal Catholics begin to do the something that they can do, the influence of the dissenters will be swept away like the wind.

Loneliness

That loyal Catholics must match the activity of Church dissenters with their own activity—and not depend on others to solve the problem for them (even if the "others" are the bishops)—is the central theme of the present book. How to do all this will be the central theme of the next book.

For now, however, let us continue to look at the emotions of the "papist" priests. In addition to the assumption of powerlessness, the loyal priests have two other feelings that deserve study. The first is the feeling of loneliness— often an overwhelming loneliness. The second is the feeling that they must somehow escape from the influence of the dissenters.

As they describe their loneliness, it becomes clear that there is one step which most of these faithful priests have never thought of taking. That step is to unite with those other priests who share their convictions. Instead, the "papist" priests remain alone. This failure of the loyal priests to unite in support of each other is a key reason that they often feel isolated. Unlike the dissenters, who are constantly forming support groups in order to build up their strength, most loyal priests are still attempting to "go it alone." Separated from each other, they are no match within their diocese for the power of an organized group of dissenters. If the "papist" priests would unite and form an active group of their own, things might be very different. However, they have not done so, perhaps because they are operating under the "assumption of powerlessness" and believe they could not be effective even as a group.

Since they remain apart from those who would support them, they often feel that nobody around them shares their attitudes. Everybody else seems to be operating as if nothing serious were happening. Better to hide one's true feelings, therefore. "To get along you go along."

Because loyal Catholics frequently consider it socially unacceptable to reveal their true feelings, they are surprised when they discover (usually by chance) that other Catholics experience similar emotions. As one example, consider an event that actually occurred at a recent meeting of a Catholic lawyers' organization. The guest speaker was a priest who was loyal to the Pope and who, unlike most "papist" priests, decided to reveal his feelings publicly. When the priest had finished his talk, there was a spontaneous reaction from the audience. One person after another arose to say that he or she had similar feelings but had never spoken about them publicly until now. The priest's statement had created an atmosphere in which it was now socially acceptable for other loyal Catholics to reveal their true attitude. When they did, they were startled to discover that something they thought nobody shared was actually a common experience.

We have been considering the lonely laymen and lonely priests. But they are not the only loyal Catholics who can feel isolated. Even a Pope can experience this feeling. (After all, Our Lord Himself felt lonely and isolated in the Garden of Gethsemene.)

In a sermon given a few days after the death of Pope Paul VI, Bishop Fulton Sheen speaks of the suffering of the Holy Father.[1] During the fifteen years of Pope Paul's Pontificate, Bishop Sheen had eleven private audiences with him and the Holy Father spoke openly to his friend about the cross he was carrying. According to the bishop, the heart of the Pope was broken by the activity of the dissenters, especially the priests and sisters who had abandoned the Church's teaching.

"I open my mail at midnight," said the Pope to Bishop Sheen. "In almost every single letter is a thorn." But the Holy Father was determined to bear this cross and to carry it with joy for the greater glory of God. In other words, the public ridicule by the dissenters of Church teaching created as much anguish in the heart of Pope Paul VI as it does today in the hearts of the "papist priests" and the faithful laity.

And, like the priests and the laity, the Holy Father suffered from a lack of support by other loyal Catholics. Or perhaps a better way to phrase it is that he suffered—not from a lack of support, but from a lack of *expressed* support. There were certainly millions and millions of Catholics who loved the Pope and who were strongly loyal to him, but out of all these millions how many saw the need to express their support publicly? How many expressed their support privately to the Pope? Unfortunately, very few. Almost every letter had a thorn. It was not that the faithful Catholics lacked concern. It was simply that the idea of writing to the Pope to express support never occurred to 99.99% of them. So the Pope was left alone to face the onslaught of the dissenters to whom the idea of writing most definitely did occur. On the one hand, he heard the constant barrage of the dissenters; on the other hand, the endless silence of loyal Catholics who, like the Apostles in the Garden, were full of good will but did not realize how crucial it was for them to supply the desperately needed support.

The pattern continues to the present day. Whenever the Pope speaks up on behalf of Catholic teaching, he is bombarded by the dissenters. As one illustration, the president of an American Catholic university, a priest who is also a supporter of the dissenters, revealed what he and his colleagues did when they thought the Vatican was about to act in a way they did not like. Some of them immediately flew to Rome to "lobby" the Pope on behalf of the dissenters, while others launched a public-relations campaign against the proposed action by the Vatican. In line with this campaign, a major television network carried a story about the dispute. The conflict was portrayed by the television network as a struggle between a "conservative" Pope and many American Catholics. No mention was made that any American Catholics might support the Pope.

While all this was happening, what were the loyal Catholics doing? How many of them flew to Rome to express their support of the Pope? How many launched a public relations campaign of their own to counter the dissenters? We do not know, but the likelihood is that private letters of support to the Pope were not much greater than they were at the time of Paul VI. As for "public relations" campaigns by loyal Catholics to counter the dissenters, if anybody did begin such an effort it was never heard of. It could be argued, of course, that the media would be reluctant to publicize such activities. Nevertheless, if enough faithful Catholics organized and began to speak up, there would soon come a time when their work simply could not be ignored even by a hostile press and television. The truth is that such activity has not occurred to the extent it must if faithful American Catholics are to be effective in defending the Pope.

When loyal Catholics unite with each other and work as hard as the dissenters, they will not only be effective in promoting Catholic doctrine but they will cease to be lonely. Instead of responding in such a constructive fashion, however, many supporters of the Pope are tempted to give up and look for a way to "escape."

In their letters to the *Homiletic and Pastoral Review*, the "papist" priests describe several methods of escape. One way is retirement (withdrawal), and two of the priests are already looking forward to it, although they are only in their late 40's and early 50's. A second route of escape is to pretend to go along with the dissenters (camouflage?), while a third method is to find a clerical fox-hole—a "priest hole"—and crawl into it (shelter). The problem with all of these methods is that they allow the individual to obtain a little personal peace but only at the price of sacrificing any opportunity to help other Catholics by promoting the Pope's teaching.

There are other forms of escape that are less dramatic than the three mentioned above. Instead of retiring completely, some loyal priests retire only from the area of religious education. If they are pastors, they concentrate on the administrative aspects of the parish, e.g., repaving the parking lot, buying a Church organ, paying off the debt. A younger "papist" priest can achieve the same effect by devoting all his time to a parish sports program or to a social action project. In both cases, the priests make a deliberate decision to stay as far away as possible from the teaching of Church doctrine because that would bring them face-to-face with the power of the dissenters. Thus, while a typical parish may contain one dissenting priest and one "papist" priest, nine times out of ten it will be the dissenting priest who runs the religious education program.

Loyal Catholics Who Are Not Suffering

We have been considering those Catholics who are suffering. Now, for a moment, let us look at the loyal Catholics who are not. Why are they free of suffering? Usually it is for one of two reasons. Either they do not know (mercifully) what is going on or they have somehow found a way to cope with the crisis, something that we will later refer to as a support system.

Let us consider the first case, those who do not know all that is going on. Perhaps some of you reading this book, hearing about the doctrines that are denied by dissident theologians, will say to yourselves: "I didn't know 95% of this was happening." If so, that is a reason you have been protected.

Sometimes even those who ought to know about the dissenters do not. About a year ago, I happened to have a discussion with two priests who served as the personal secretaries to the diocesan bishop. At the request of a seminary professor, the bishop had invited a prominent theological dissenter to address all the priests. Amazingly, neither of the monsignors who served as the bishop's secretaries had ever read the works of this dissenter. They had only the vaguest knowledge of what he was saying. Yet it was their responsibility to prepare the bishop's letters of response to those laity who did know about the dissenter and who were writing to protest the fact that a priest who attacked so many Church teachings was being given such an opportunity.

In other words, loyal Catholics often do not suffer because they have little contact with the dissenters. The dissenters themselves frequently realize that they will lose the opportunity to influence many Catholics unless they can somehow force these Catholics to listen to them. That is the reason that (surprisingly enough) attendance at programs given by dissenters is sometimes made compulsory within a parish or diocese.

It may seem as if the failure to read is not a good thing. In one sense that is certainly true. But, in the present Church climate, the fact that many Catholics do not read theological works protects them from a great amount of confusion, if not downright heresy. In this regard, I think of a comment that G. K. Chesterton once made upon visiting America and walking down Broadway. He wrote: "What a glorious garden of wonders this would be to anyone who is lucky enough to be unable to read." Explaining, he pointed out that a visitor who did not know English would see the brilliant lights of Broadway. He would observe everything lit up like a comet and would realize that a message was being flashed. Not knowing English, he would assume that the glittering message being flashed must be something wonderful and inspiring like "Government of the people, for the people, and by the people." As Chesterton remarked, the visitor would be a little shaken if he could read. Then he would know that the glittering message in front of him was "Tang tonic today, tang tonic tomorrow, tang tonic all the time." He would also know that the equally brilliant message across the street did not stand for "Give me liberty or give me death," but was actually an advertisement informing the public that "Skyoline has gout beaten to a frazzle." As long as the language remains foreign, one is protected from the junk behind the glitter, but one is also likely to assume that the glitter must be something important.

In writing these words, I am thinking about the "glitter" of certain colleges that call themselves Catholic but that are actually strongholds of dissent. These places still retain all of their surface brilliance. Unfortunately, those who attend these institutions usually end up learning not Catholic doctrine, but the theological equivalent of "Skyoline has gout beaten to a frazzle."

Let us return, however, to those loyal Catholics who are not suffering because they have not personally experienced the activity of the dissenters. Perhaps they still live in one of those orthodox parishes where the problem of dissent does not exist. Or, if it does exist in some parts of the parish, they themselves do not come in contact with it.

It is very good that such Catholics are protected from theological "junk." It might even be desirable to leave them that way—except for two things. First, the dissenters are unlikely to leave such Catholics alone forever. Second, while lack of knowledge about a problem can protect you at times, it also means that you cannot act to solve the problem. If you do not read English, you will not be adversely affected by the glittering sign on Broadway. You will also be unable to change the silly message into one that is truly important. In the same way, loyal Catholics who are unaware of the activities of the dissenters retain their personal reverence for the Church but are usually unable to help the Church overcome the dissent within Her midst.

The second kind of loyal but non-suffering Catholics are those who are aware of dissent but who have found a way to cope. Basically, there are two such ways. As described previously, the first "way to cope" is to make a conscious decision to withdraw from the struggle either by seeking retirement or by finding a religious "foxhole" of some kind. But there is also a second "way to cope," a way that enables loyal Catholics not only to continue in the battle for Catholic teaching but even to intensify their efforts rather than withdraw. What is this second way? It is for faithful Catholics to build their own support systems. Therefore, let us turn our attention to the question of support systems since the formation of such groups is the one means by which orthodox Catholics can help *both* themselves *and* the Church in general.

NOTES

[1] The quotation that follows is from the cassette tape of Archbishop Sheen referred to in the footnote of Chapter 1.

4.
The Need for Support Systems

What is a support system? As the phrase itself might indicate, it is an organization of some kind. The purpose of the organization is to help us to live in a certain way ("support"). Support systems can be either physical or social. A "physical" support system is a machine (e.g., a boat, a plane, an air-conditioner). A "social" system is a group of people (e.g., a family, a Church group, an association formed to achieve a goal). Whether they are physical or social, support systems operate in a similar way. Therefore, in order to understand the reason that the support systems within the Catholic Church are failing, let us begin by looking at the simplest kind of support system—the physical.

What do boats, planes, and air-conditioners have in common? They all enable us to do something that would otherwise be impossible. To put it another way, they give us the power to resist the pressure of the outside world. There are certain conditions that exist in the world surrounding us. We can call them "forces" or "pressures" or "currents." Perhaps the best word is "climate" or "environment." The environment of the world surrounding us would ordinarily affect us in a certain way. A physical support system, however, changes all this. It enables us to resist the outside environment, even to be unaffected by it.

Take an air-conditioner and, provided that the machine is working properly and we are close enough to it, we are no longer affected by the heat. Instead, we feel cool. The air-conditioner, a physical support system, has protected us from the outside environment and created a more comfortable climate for us.

As an air-conditioner protects us from the outside environment of heat, so a boat protects us from the outside environment of water. A boat enables us to do what would otherwise be impossible—to travel over water without sinking. Ordinarily, the physical force that scientists call "gravity" would cause us to sink. A boat is a support system that enables us to resist the pressure of gravity. A plane serves a similar purpose with respect to travel through the air.

It should be noted that a specially constructed support system is not needed when the outside environment is helpful rather than hostile. In that case, the environment itself provides the necessary support. We do not need a boat to travel by land because the ground itself supports us. We do not need an air-conditioner when the weather is 65 rather than 90. But whenever we want to resist the outside environment an effective support system is needed. Without such a support system, there is no defense against the outside environment. We must inevitably sink in the water and swelter in the heat.

Social Support Systems

In considering support systems, we have been concentrating on physical machines such as boats or air-conditioners. Let us now look at social support systems.

A social support system must be composed of a person or group of persons. All of us have experienced how necessary it is to have somebody with whom we can share the most important moments of our lives. Otherwise, even the good times seem lonely. The help of such persons is especially needed whenever we face a crisis.

In a good marriage, a husband and wife play a crucial role in supporting each other. If one of them comes down with a serious physical illness or experiences great tension because of difficulties that have developed at work, the other party is always there to listen, to advise, and above all, to love. If their marriage is blessed with children, their sons and daughters will also become an indispensable part of the social support system that we call the family.

In addition to the family, there are other kinds of social support systems. Our friends can give us invaluable support. Or, we can join organizations designed to help us in a certain area. If we love music, we can join a music club. If we are enthusiastic about chess, we can become a member of a chess club. A person with an interest has a natural tendency to seek out people with similar interests. Why? The basic reason is that association with such like-minded people provides a kind of support system that helps us to go forward in the direction we desire.

What was said about physical systems is also true of social systems. They are especially needed when the outside environment is hostile. The worse the environment, the stronger the support system must become.

The other day I read a story about a man whom I will call John Smith. He was writing about a difficult period of his life when he felt overwhelmed by problems that arose in connection with his business. According to John Smith, he could never have survived without the constant support of his wife and family. This is not an unusual experience.

For a support system to work, it must remain solid. If only a single part fails, that can be enough to wreck the value of the entire system due to the intricate relationships among the elements of the system. Imagine a boat that is thirty feet long. Now imagine that a three-inch hole develops in the bottom of the boat. Will this cause the boat to sink? Yes—unless the damage is repaired in time. Even though 99% of the boat's surface remains as solid as ever, the failure of 1% destroys the support system and makes the boat incapable of resisting the outside environment.

It is the same with the plane and the air-conditioner. A plane has literally thousands of parts and an air-conditioner also has many parts. If only a single key part fails, the plane cannot fly and the air-conditioner cannot cool. It makes no difference that 90% of the parts continue to work well.

Social support systems have a similar need for solidarity. Suppose, for instance, that a family becomes wracked with internal controversy. Instead of being a support, the family is now a place of sharp conflict. Perhaps the problem begins with only one person. All the other people in the family remain the same, but one individual becomes an alcoholic or a drug-addict. Is this individual the only person who is affected? No, the entire family is thrown into turmoil. Like the physical support systems, like the boat and the air-conditioner, a hole in one part can disrupt the entire family support system.

To cope with the problem, the family in crisis may seek outside help. If the difficulty is alcoholism, the drinker in the family may join Alcoholics Anonymous, a support system to help alcoholics overcome their drinking problems. Meanwhile, the non-drinkers in the family are joining another kind of support system, an organization set up specifically to aid the families of alcoholics.

The Catholic Church

How does this all apply to the Catholic Church? The outside environment, i.e., the culture in which we live, is hostile to many Catholic beliefs and practices. Until recently Catholics had a strong support system that enabled them to resist such pressure. With the collapse of this support system, there is now (as some pollsters delight in pointing out) little difference between the beliefs and attitudes of many Catholics and the beliefs and attitudes of their non-Catholic neighbors. Catholics have become "like everybody else" in being affected by the heat.

Once we realize that solidarity is necessary for an effective support system, we can understand the reason that the support systems within the Catholic Church failed so suddenly. In the support systems created by the Church to promote her teaching on faith and morals (Catholic schools, religious education programs, parishes, newspapers, etc.) there continue to be many loyal Catholics. These priests, religious, and lay people are like the part of the boat that continues to remain solid. However, to puncture the support system, to render it incapable of resisting the outside environment, all that is required is the appearance of a few holes.

There are still some parishes and schools where the dissenters have not yet made their presence felt. These places continue to be effective support systems in promoting Catholic teaching. In most Church institutions, however, there are enough dissenters to put holes in the system, to make Catholic schools and parishes the religious equivalent of a leaky rowboat. When loyal Catholics appeal to the bishops to remove dissenters from key Church positions, what they are really requesting is that the "holes in the boat" be fixed so that the Church's support systems will be effective once more. Unfortunately, despite the appeals of faithful Catholics, and despite similar calls for action by the Vatican itself, it seems unlikely that most bishops will take the necessary steps to do this. We have already discussed some of the reasons for their inaction (e.g., the fear of many bishops that such action would create an open revolt or the belief that the problem is so big that the individual bishop is relatively powerless) and we will return to this subject in a future chapter.

For now, let us simply state the truth as honestly as possible. Unless the bishops totally reverse what they have been doing since Vatican II, they will not be taking the steps that are necessary to repair the Church's support systems. While the bishops will continue to express their personal support of Church doctrines, little or nothing will be done to check the influence of the dissenters within Church institutions. The blunt truth is that if loyal Catholics are waiting for the bishops to fix the holes in the boat they may be waiting until hell freezes over.

Is there, then, no hope for faithful Catholics? Yes, there is hope. There is most definitely an answer to the problem. Instead of relying on the bishops for actions that will not be forthcoming, loyal Catholics must create their own support systems to promote Church doctrine—systems that are effective in gaining support for the Church's teaching on faith and morals. In other words, faithful Catholics must do for themselves what in previous ages was done for them by the official institutions of the parish or diocese.

This does not mean that faithful Catholics should abandon the official institutions of the Church to the dissenters. To the contrary, loyal Catholics should be as active as possible in the official institutions in order to check the influence of the dissenters and promote orthodox Catholic teaching. However, it should be understood clearly that the functioning of these official institutions has changed from what it was in the past. In pre-Vatican II days, these official institutions were the support systems for Catholics; the places that give loyal Catholics the strength to fight for their beliefs in the world. In that period, Catholics could receive all the support they needed from the official institutions set up by the Church for this purpose. There was no need for additional support systems. Today things are different. Because the dissenters have wrought such havoc within the Church, the official Church institutions of the present day are often the battleground itself, the arena in which loyal Catholics must struggle to advance the Church's teaching against the sneers and the ridicule of the dissenters.

Faithful Catholics must come to realize that the battleground cannot also be the training ground. Just as the members of a family ripped apart by alcoholism must seek additional support both to strengthen them personally and to help them restore the family to its former health, so orthodox Catholics must build their own support systems to strengthen them as individuals in the faith and to give them the necessary help to participate in the official Church institutions and work for the true Catholic teaching.

It is not easy to do all this. It would be far easier simply to abandon the family in crisis. Some Catholics have chosen this course by joining "traditionalist" churches. In that way, they avoid the influence of the dissenters. In doing this, however, one risks abandoning the Pope and the Catholic Church that we believe Christ Himself created. It is similar to abandoning your parents or your children because it pains you to see them in suffering. You can avoid the pain by leaving them, but how does such desertion help the people you are supposed to love? If you truly love them, if you are thinking of others rather than yourself, you will find a way to endure your personal suffering (even though you yourself may have to seek the support of other people to do this) in order to be present to help your loved ones in their moment of crisis. That is the kind of love loyal Catholics must give to the Holy Father in the present Church crisis, and they need the constant prayers and personal support of other like-minded Catholics in order to do this.

In summary, there are two mistakes that loyal Catholics should avoid. The first mistake is not to build their own support systems, to assume that the official institutions of the Church will be a support system as they were in the past. If this mistake occurs, then, as Bishop Sheen warned with respect to "Catholic" colleges, those who come to the official institutions as loyal but unwary Catholics will often be scandalized and lose their faith. The second mistake is for orthodox Catholics to build their own support systems and then to withdraw from active participation in the official diocesan or parish programs. If this happens, there will be nobody to check the power of the dissenters in the official programs and orthodox Catholics will lose the opportunity to assist many of their fellow Catholics whose beliefs are being undermined by what is taking place in their parish, school, or diocese.

A "Cognitive Minority"

In discussing the importance of strong support systems to promote Catholic beliefs, we have been assuming that the "outside environment," the general society in which we live, is hostile to these beliefs. Why is this so? The word "hostile" does not necessarily imply a personal bitterness or antagonism of society towards the Catholic Church. This may well be present in a "hostile" climate, but again it may not. What "hostile" basically means is that the environment is such that it is very difficult for Catholic beliefs to survive. It is like a summer plant in the cold of winter. The cold does not consciously "hate" the plant. Nevertheless, the plant will almost certainly die because the climate is unfavorable to its existence (unless, of course, the plant can obtain the heat it needs from a source other than the outside environment, i.e., a support system).

In today's world, Catholics belong to what some sociologists describe as a "cognitive minority." The word "cognitive" refers to beliefs. The word "minority" reminds us that most of the people in our society do not share these beliefs. As a general rule, it is relatively easy to believe something if the conviction is shared by the "cognitive majority" around us. That is like being a summer plant in summer. On the other hand, it is extraordinarily difficult to believe something if the conviction is rejected by the "cognitive majority" around us.

Suppose you meet a girl named Betty. Your initial judgment is that Betty is a very fine person. But suppose that three of your close friends have also reached a judgment about Betty. What happens to the belief you have found if,

(1) all of your friends agree with you;
(2) all of your friends disagree with you;
(3) two of your friends agree with you but one disagrees;
(4) two disagree but one agrees.

The more your belief is reinforced the easier it is for you to maintain it. If everybody is reinforcing your conviction, then it will probably never occur to you to doubt it. If a majority but not everybody supports you, then it will still be relatively easy to continue your belief, but it will not be quite as easy as it was when all of your friends were confirming your judgment. If only a minority backs you, then belief becomes more difficult. Finally, if nobody at all supports you, then it becomes extremely difficult to maintain your belief. Consciously or unconsciously, you are under a great amount of pressure to change your views to conform with the public opinion around you. You are on the defensive. You will continually have to resist a doubting voice within you that is saying: "How can I be right when everybody else believes the opposite?"

Although the phrase "cognitive majority" may be new, the Catholic Church has long held that the attitudes of other people can influence us strongly for good or for evil. Over and over again throughout her history, the Church has urged Catholics to avoid "occasions of sin", i.e., those persons, places, or things that tempt us to evil. How often have we been taught that bad companions can lead us into sin, while good companions, on the other hand, can encourage us in virtue. Although the Church respects free will, she has always urged us not to trust in our free will alone. No, we must try to avoid temptation (that is, those persons or situations that make it more difficult for us to follow the teachings of Jesus Christ and His Church on faith and morals) while building up our association with the good, that is, persons or situations that strengthen us in our adherence to Catholic teaching.

When the Church's support system was solid, it protected Catholics from the social pressures of the outside world. The result? Most Catholics believed strongly in the Church's teachings even if these teachings were rejected by the "cognitive majority" outside.

With the general collapse of the Church's support systems, all this has changed. If we are to believe the sociologists, most "Catholics" are increasingly becoming "like everyone else" both in their beliefs and in their moral practice. These "Catholics" no longer have any effective means to resist the "cognitive majority," so they tend to conform to the prevalent public opinion. On faith and morals, they believe and do whatever the "cognitive majority" in the outside world believes and does.

Does this mean that such Catholics reject every Church teaching? Not necessarily. They usually reject only those Church teachings that the "cognitive majority" in the outside world rejects. it can sometimes be forgotten that there are certain Church teachings that the "cognitive majority" may actually support. For example, at the present time in the United States, the public-opinion polls reveal that the overwhelming majority of Americans believe in the existence of God and in life after death. Therefore, the overwhelming majority of American Catholics presently believe in the existence of God and in life after death, and they will probably continue to hold this belief as long as the American "cognitive majority' supports it. However, if the "cognitive majority" were to change its view and deny these beliefs, it is likely that many "Catholics" would soon follow suit.

The Cross

If the "cognitive majority" in the outside world does not reject all Catholic teaching, what does it repudiate? Above all, *the Cross*. The majority of people in our modern society would like to keep the consoling part of Christ's teaching, but not the part that involves sacrifice and suffering. Belief in life after death is a Christian doctrine that is comforting, especially when we realize that our moments on earth may be drawing to a close. There is an old saying that there are no atheists in foxholes.

While the consoling doctrines continue to be popular, in contrast, the doctrines that require sacrifice are widely rejected. Consider the Church's teaching on contraception, abortion, and divorce—teachings repudiated by the "cognitive majority." What all these teachings have in common is that they require a considerable sacrifice to follow them. The attitude of the modern world can be summarized as follows: "Christ could not possibly want us to operate under such hardship. It is fine to have children and it is fine to remain married to your husband or wife, as long as you find it helpful to do so. However, if it would be difficult for you to have a child, then it is permissible to practice contraception or abortion. If it would be difficult for you to remain married to your partner, then it is permissible to sever the relationship and choose another partner who would be more helpful and more consoling. The basic rule is that you should always have a right to do what is necessary to avoid unpleasantness and suffering."

The only problem with such an attitude is that it is simply not the religion founded by Jesus Christ. Our Lord Himself tells us that if we wish to be His disciples we must take up the Cross and follow Him. This invitation of Our Lord has never been popular. In Christ's own day, there were multitudes who wanted to be with Him in the moments of triumph but only a handful who stood by Him in the moments of suffering. Even the trusted Apostles of Jesus originally thought they could have love without sacrifice. When Our Lord told Peter that the Son of Man would suffer and die, Peter refused to believe it. The Apostle, assuming he knew more than the Master, insisted that what Our Lord had revealed could not possibly be the case. Jesus had to rebuke Peter sternly, even calling him "Satan," which means "adversary." Very harsh words, but Our Lord did not hesitate to speak them because it was vital for His followers to realize that one cannot have Christianity without the Cross.

Peter later repented, of course. He had the humility to see his faults and admit them. However, during the time that Peter thought He knew more than Christ, his attitude was remarkably similar to that of the dissenting theologians of today. Like the rebellious Peter, the dissenting theologians "know it all." They simply refuse to listen if the Vicar of Christ says anything contrary to their views, as Peter would not hear Christ. Like Peter, they have turned their relationship with Christ and His Church upside down. In this new topsy-turvy world, they intend to "educate" the Pope as the Apostle sought to teach Christ. Finally, their basic message is the same as that of the rebellious Peter, namely, that those teachings involving hardship cannot possibly be true and should be discarded as soon as possible. As Peter was Christ's "adversary," so these individuals are the Church's "adversary" not only refusing to listen to the Pope themselves but doing everything in their power to prevent other Catholics from listening.

The love and faith of loyal Catholics must change all this. By our prayers, by our work, and by our sacrifices we can overcome the scandal of the dissenters and help other Catholics to rediscover their birthright—the Full Christ, the True Christ, the Christ of Love Who is also the Christ of the Cross.

5.
A Summary of the Dissenters' Tactics

In the last three chapters we have concentrated on the difficulties that faithful Catholics experience because of the assault on Catholic teaching by the dissenters. Now let us look at the dissenters themselves, beginning with a study of their tactics. Throughout both the first book and this one, we have considered the strategy employed by the dissenters to advance their own views and to undercut the authority of the Pope and traditional Church teaching. Before adding a few additional points, here is a brief summary of those "dissenter strategies" that have already been discussed, along with references to the chapters in both books where the discussion occurred.

Strategy I: To Build Their Own "Power Base"

A. create support groups with other dissenters . . . a "network" to assist the growth of dissent and to help any dissenter in trouble (Book 2, Chapter 3);

B. occupy key posts within the Church . . . become established in Church institutions (schools, newspapers, etc.) created to promote the Faith and use them for the opposite purpose of promoting dissent and propagandizing against the official Church teaching (Book 2, Chapter 1 and 3);

C. use sympathetic contacts in the secular media (Book 2, Chapter 3);

D. seek converts at every opportunity . . . sell dissent (Book 2, Chapter 3).

Strategy II: Prevent Interference

A. General strategy:

1) leave those people alone who keep silent about dissent and strike back at anybody who attempts to check dissent (Book 2, Chapter 3);

2) create a bandwagon effect by claiming that the overwhelming weight of public opinion is on the side of dissent (Book 2 Chapter 2);

3) arouse sympathy for dissent by

    a. stating that dissenters are in the middle between the extremists on both sides (Book 2, Chapter 2);

    b. using warm and sympathetic words to describe the position held by dissenters but cold and harsh sounding words to describe the official Church position (Book 2, Chapter 2);

    c. relying not so much on a logical approach but on an emotional sales technique of identifying dissent with qualities people want (Book 2, Chapter 2).

B. Strategy toward the bishops:

1) long-range goal—get bishops to speak out for dissent. To achieve this, seek constantly to meet with bishops; quietly lobby them (Book 2, Chapter 3);

2) short-range goal—get bishops to leave dissenters alone by creating great uproar if bishops intervene (Book 2, Chapter 3).

C. Strategy toward the Vatican itself:

1) write constantly to the Pope. Continually "lobby" the Vatican to "back down." Try to create the impression that almost everyone is with the dissenters and nobody agrees with the Pope (Book 2, Chapter 3);

2) tell Church authorities that there will be wonderful effects if only the Church will abandon Her traditional teaching (Book 2, Chapter 2).

D. Strategy toward the Catholic laity:

1) promote the view that dissent is related to advancement in scholarship (even if this is not the case). Tell laity who hesitate to accept dissent that they are not competent to question it, and, if they wish to be knowledgeable, they must accept "change" and "current thinking," that is, the position of the dissenters (Book 2, Chapter 1, Book 1, Chapter 7);

2) if laity persists in defending Church teaching, dissenting theological "experts" should use their superior knowledge of facts to make the loyal laity appear uninformed or ridiculous. Do not hesitate to twist the facts to

achieve this goal. Particular techniques to use are:

    a. claim falsely that Second Vatican Council justified dissent (Book 1, Chapter 1);

    b. tell Catholics they should be insulted to have to obey "blindly" the Pope's authority (Book 1, Chapter 3);

    c) confuse the personal talents of the Pope with the authority of his office and imply that Catholics need only follow the Pope if his personal expertise merits it (Book 1, Chapter 3);

    d) promote the view that one can "pick and choose" among Church teachings (Book 1, Chapter 3);

    e) use technical words that have two or more meanings and use them in a vague way or in a manner different from that intended by the Church (Book 1, Chapter 5). By confusing the meaning of the word "infallibility," create the impression that all teachings of the "ordinary" magisterium are unsure and, therefore, optional (Book 1, Chapter 4). Create a similar mix-up with words such as "ordinary" and "authority," confusing the authority of the office with the authority of the "expert" (Book 1, Chapter 3);

    f) do not distinguish between doctrinal statements and disciplinary statements, between direct teachings and "obiter dicta," between final authoritative decisions intended to be binding and provisional teachings. Basing statements on this confusion, "prove" that Church decisions in the past have been "erroneous" and conclude that ones at present may be erroneous also (Book 1, Chapter 5);

    g) claim that particular Church teachings "only began in the eleventh century," therefore, they are not basic to the Church and can be discarded as man-made (Book 1, Chapter 6).

E. Strategy toward those theologians who defend Church teaching:

    1) avoid debate with defenders of the Pope's teaching, especially those who are knowledgeable and articulate (Book 2, Chapter 2);

    2) seek as much as possible to diminish the influence of theologians loyal to the Pope and opposed to the dissenters. If in an administrative position to do so, do not hesitate to silence such loyal theologians and ban their books (Book 1, Chapter 7).

Having briefly summarized some of the strategies of the dissenters already discussed, let us look at five other tactics that play an important role in their success.

First Tactic—"Inside dissenters" help "outside dissenters."

Although it was probably not consciously planned by the dissenters, they have developed a good balance of "outside" and "inside" men. What do I mean by these terms? The "outside" men are those who speak up and publicly attack Church teaching and the authority of the Pope. They say whatever is on their minds, and they do not hesitate to denounce all who disagree with them. What we are describing here is a kind of personality. The personality of these "outside" dissenters is such that they do not even pretend to accept Church teaching. Instead, they publicly attempt to diminish that teaching.

The "outside" men do not get close to the bishops because they are constantly denouncing them. The typical bishop or other Church authority stays as far away as possible from "outside" individuals. That is the reason they are "outside." What they are able to accomplish, however, is to generate tremendous controversy. Church authorities are often fearful of their ability to do this.

Left to themselves, the "outside" people, for all the noise they generate, would probably have little effect upon the Church. In the present situation, however, they are supported by a network of "inside" people. We might refer to these "insiders" as "politicians" because, unlike those who are blunt and outspoken, a politician frequently does not tell you exactly what is on his mind. Instead, he guards his public comments and works quietly behind the scenes toward a particular goal. The "inside" men are eager to work with the bishops. They will try to avoid public action that would embarrass those in authority. However, since they are personally sympathetic to doctrinal dissent, the "insiders" will use every opportunity they can to promote it.

For instance, there are numerous priest-"theologians" who dissented from the Pope and then left the priesthood. The vocal opponents of the Pope are "outside" people. Nevertheless, it is customary in many dioceses to invite such "outside" people to speak in parishes and religious education courses and even to write in Catholic newspapers. They serve on the faculty of Catholic universities, their books are constantly read, they sell thousands of copies of these books to Church institutions. Who arranges for all this? It is the "inside" people, those who are in charge of such programs. These individuals do not themselves leave the priesthood. They usually do not denounce the Pope publicly, for if they did, they might well be removed from their positions of influence. No, they avoid giving local Church authorities any such embarrassment. Yet they make an indispensable contribution to dissent by providing the "outside people" with an audience and a power that the outsiders could otherwise not possess. In this way, the "outside" people and the "inside" people work together in the promotion of dissent.

Second Tactic—Support administration but attack doctrine

An important tactic often pursued by "inside" dissenters is to be most helpful to the bishop on administrative matters. Some insiders achieve a position of diocesan influence by making themselves practically indispensable on administrative questions. They challenge the doctrinal authority of the Pope, but not the administrative authority of the local bishop.

An illustration of how this works occurred several years ago in a parish. The pastor of the parish was supposed to be a "conservative" priest who would be unfavorable to dissent. Yet he was in need of priests to come in from outside to assist him at the Sunday Masses. Two different kinds of priests came forward. The first priest was a professor of theology who dissented openly from many key teachings of the Church. In sermon after sermon, this priest began to "update" the people of the parish on the reasons that traditional Church doctrines were no longer valid. At the same time, however, he was most willing to accept the administrative power of the pastor and never challenged the pastor's practical decisions. Whatever Masses the pastor wished to assign to this dissident theologian were accepted without question. If the pastor wanted him to come on some other occasion, the dissident theologian would always be there. He could not have been more helpful on administration.

The outcome? The pastor willingly kept him on and turned a deaf ear to any parishioners who questioned the dissenting priest's sermons. "You must be mistaken," the pastor would reply. "Fr. X is sometimes technical, but he would never say that." The only problem with this response was that it was not true; Fr. X was indeed saying it.

Meanwhile, a second priest came to the parish. This priest was as doctrinally loyal as one could imagine. Nevertheless, he sometimes made decisions himself on administrative matters and did not ask the pastor for permission. For example, this priest wanted to have a layman read the Epistle even at daily Masses. That was not the custom of the parish. However, the priest went ahead with his idea. He even put an additional chair on the altar near the lectern. Before each daily Mass, he invited a member of the laity to come up and read the Epistle. When the pastor learned of the situation he became very angry. How dare a visiting priest move chairs around the altar and change the customs of the parish without obtaining the pastor's permission! The pastor quickly took steps to remove from his parish the priest who had challenged his authority on administrative matters.

Is this an isolated occurrence? I do not believe so. For reasons we will discuss later, local authorities frequently crack down vigorously on those who dissent on administrative matters but leave to their own devices those who accept administrative policies but challenge the authority of the Pope on faith and morals. It is this tolerance of doctrinal dissent that has enabled many "inside men" to make great progress.

In contrast to the "inside" supporters of dissent, those who wish to defend Church doctrine often seem to be "outside." They are "outside" in the sense that they do not occupy key positions in the Church's administrative structure. For whatever reasons, the loyal Catholics do not seem to have developed an effective network of "inside" supporters to match the network developed by the dissenters. Despite the personal views of those administrative officials who support Church doctrine (and there are certainly many Church administrators who do support the official Church teaching), they do not seem to promote the Pope's views as successfully as the "inside dissenters" promote the views of those who oppose the Pope.

Third Tactic—Find ways to promote dissent without saying so.

Like the pastor in the example given above, many bishops do not act when orthodox Catholics outside the administrative structure protest the activities of "closet" doctrinal dissenters who have made themselves administratively indispensable. Instead, these bishops deny that the problem really exists.

However, there are other bishops who do attempt to act. How do "inside dissenters" protect themselves in such a situation? Usually they duck. They assure the bishop of their own personal orthodoxy. Remember that "inside men" do not have to oppose Church doctrine publicly. All they have to do is provide a forum for the "outside dissenters" who will do all the public denunciation necessary to undermine the Church's teaching. Therefore, when an administrator sympathetic to the dissenters is questioned by the bishop, he or she can respond: "Of course, I do not oppose the

Pope's teaching. All that I am doing is what educators all over the country are doing, allowing recognized experts to present their views. Academic freedom demands this. However, should their views disturb you, your Excellency, it might be helpful to recall that these experts come from outside of our diocese. Therefore, you are not responsible in any way for what they say or do since the experts are not under your authority."

Recently one "inside dissenter" prepared material on the birth control question for a diocesan Pre-Cana program. He began with two paragraphs from Pope Paul VI. While the paragraphs set forth the Church's position, the few sentences from the Pope that were quoted did not allow an adequate presentation of that position. After the "view of the Pope" came no less than five pages of material explaining in detail the position of the "theological experts"—all of whom were dissenters. No theologian supporting the Pope was even mentioned.

Such a presentation is the equivalent of "brain-washing" on behalf of the dissenters. But one has to use the phrase "the equivalent of" because, you see, the diocesan official who prepared the material never said directly: "I favor the dissenters." Therefore, he could assure his bishop that he never had and never would make a pro-contraception statement. In fact, he could even assure the bishop that he always presented the official Church teaching first, and only afterwards proceeded ("as all who value academic freedom must") to report other views.

If necessary, an "inside dissenter" can go a step farther. Instead of avoiding all reference to his personal opinion, he can even praise the Pope's position, but so weakly and half-heartedly that his audience will in reality be led in the opposite direction.

As the old saying goes, it is definitely possible to "damn with faint praise." In this regard, I once heard a well-known theatre critic comment that, if he really wanted to hurt a play, the best approach was not to attack it directly but to praise it lukewarmly as "fair" and "adequate." His reasoning? If he attacked the play vigorously, some of his readers might dismiss his review as prejudiced and go to the play anyway. In contrast, if he appeared to be ever so slightly favorable to the play, he could avoid the impression of prejudice. Then nobody would go to the play because no one wants to spend time and money attending a play that is only "fair" and "adequate." Certain Church dissenters know all about this technique of "damning with faint praise." It enables them to duck any problems from the bishop by saying: "Bishop, not only do I not oppose the Church's teaching but I even made a statement in favor of it."

Fourth Tactic—Whenever possible, hide behind the bishop.

In the last few paragraphs, we have been considering the situation where the bishop himself asks questions of the "inside dissenter." However, if the questions are raised by anybody else, a dissenter often finds it convenient to hide behind the "apron strings" of the local bishop. "This is Bishop X's approved program. So, if you question it, you are actually questioning him."

Fifth Tactic—Banning orthodoxy for stylistic reasons.

A final tactic of many "inside dissenters" is to create their own "index," their own list of forbidden books and speakers. The prohibited books and speakers are those that emphasize orthodox Catholic doctrine in their presentations. In attempting to reduce the influence of those defending Church teaching, supporters of dissent are careful not to put things that bluntly, especially since they have justified their own promotion of dissent by appealing to freedom of discussion. Instead, it will be said that the works of orthodox Catholics must be barred from parish or diocesan programs for reasons of style or "competence," on grounds that the traditional Catholic presentation is "out of date" or "no longer meaningful to the Catholic people." In this way, inside dissenters can censor all they want, while protecting their image by acting in the name of newness and competence rather than in the name of what they are actually doing, i. e., practicing thought control in an attempt to keep Catholics from hearing presentations that give strong support to the authority of the Pope and traditional Catholic teaching.

6.
Doctrine—A Reflection In A Mirror or Shadow On A Wall

Why do the dissenters reject so many Church teachings, including doctrines that the Church herself has declared to be of the utmost importance? In addition to the explanations discussed in other chapters of this book, there is one reason so crucial that it deserves a special chapter of its own. If we understand this reason, we will also comprehend in a much better way the struggle that is taking place within today's Church. *The dissenters reject many Church doctrines because they have a notion of doctrine that is very different from that possessed by the official Church and orthodox Catholics.*

Almost everything done by the dissenters reflects this very different notion of doctrine. To understand it, let us consider the difference between a reflection in a mirror and a shadow on a wall.

Doctrine: A Mirror of God's Life

Imagine that you are looking into a good mirror. What you see is a detailed picture of your face as it actually is. You see your eyelashes, the slope of your nose, the freckles on your face, the shape of your chin. When you open your mouth, you can even see your tongue and your white front teeth, including that empty space where a tooth was knocked out last year.

Without a mirror, you could never see yourself in this way since it is not possible for you to look at your face directly. Technically, of course, what you are seeing is not yourself but the image that is in the mirror. However, this does not bother you because you know that the mirror is accurate.

Through the mirror, you can see your face as it actually is, and see it in detail. What you see is something *objective*, that is, something that actually exists. It is *not* something *subjective*, that is, something you yourself make up out of your imagination.

Because the picture in the mirror is a reflection of something that truly exists outside of your mind, you do not have the power to change it whenever you desire. Thus, you cannot jump out of bed one morning and announce to the world: "Today I'm not in the mood for freckles. Therefore—presto!—the freckles no longer exist." They are, and they will continue to be, unless you change the outside reality by going to a cosmetic surgeon and having them removed.

Now it would be very different if the picture were not a reflection of reality but a drawing that you yourself had created out of your own imagination. In that case, you could add or subtract whatever you wished. If the picture were a creation of your own mind, the important questions for you to consider would be these: "What do I want to do? What is meaningful to me?"

In dealing with an outside reality, however, the important question must always be "Is it true?," not "Is it meaningful to me?" If the freckles on your face actually exist, then they will appear in any accurate mirror-picture even if you yourself regard freckles as irrelevant. If the freckles do not exist, then they will not be in the picture, even if you yourself consider freckles to be the most meaningful of facial features. The picture in the mirror is a reflection of what actually exists, not a reflection of your own desires or emotion.

Just as a mirror reflects your face as it actually exists, so the Church has always believed that Catholic doctrine reflects God's life as it actually exists. We know about God's life only because He has chosen to reveal Himself to us. What God tells us is true and it always will be true. As St. Paul writes in the Bible: "Jesus Christ is the same yesterday, today, and forever. Do not be carried away by all kinds of strange teaching." (Hebrews 13:8-9)

Human beings have no power whatever to change what God has revealed. If there is a clash between God's Word and our own desires, then it is we who must change, not God's Word. If a teaching of Christ appears meaningless to us, then it is our perception that is faulty and not the Christian teaching.

Since God is infinite, we will never know everything about His life. Nevertheless, God has been very, very generous to us. He has revealed so much that we know many things with certainty and in detail. In that sense

Christian doctrine can be compared to a reflection in a mirror, clear and detailed in many respects, and (even more important) not a creation of man's own imagination but an independent reality that is true.

The Shadow on the Wall

What we have just described is the way that the Church has historically regarded Catholic doctrine, and the way that orthodox Catholics as well as the official Church continue to regard it. But how do many of the dissenters look at Christian teaching? To answer this question, let us consider a second example, a shadow on a wall.

Some months ago I saw a quiz game that involved a shadow on the wall. In the game, a number of contestants were challenged to guess what an individual named Smith actually looked like. The contestant who came closest would win a prize. The game-players were not allowed to look at Smith directly. They were not even told whether Smith was a man or a woman. The only clue presented was a vague shadow of Smith flashed upon the wall. Since little or nothing could be deduced from this indistinct shadow, the contest depended upon luck rather than skill.

Imagine yourself in such a situation. All you know with certainty is that a person named Smith is out there somewhere. Nothing of Smith's actual features is revealed to you. Since you are interested in Smith, however, you make up a picture of Smith out of your own imagination. In doing this, you give Smith whatever features you desire. Other people do the same. As a result, there are now hundreds of pictures of Smith in circulation, each of them different. The actual Smith, of course, cannot possibly resemble all of these pictures, but since nobody can know what the actual Smith looks like, one picture is as good as another. Choose whatever picture you wish. Select anything that is helpful to you; anything that you personally find meaningful. If you change your opinion tomorrow, then alter the picture accordingly. What has an impact on you is right for you. What does not is wrong for you. You yourself are the sole and final judge. In the same way, other people are the sole and final judges of the pictures they choose.

If you were to substitute the word "God" for "Smith," you would have a good idea of the way that many dissenters regard Catholic teaching. Instead of believing that doctrine involves a revelation from God Himself and is objectively true, these dissenters believe that doctrine is basically a creation of man's religious imagination. According to dissenters, this can be true both of beliefs regarding faith (e.g., the doctrine that Christ is God or the doctrine that Jesus is truly present in the Eucharist), and of beliefs regarding moral practice (e.g., the teaching that adultery and abortion represent acts that a follower of Christ should never undertake). Since all of these doctrines are judged to come from man's own religious imagination, two conclusions immediately follow. First, any of these teachings can be abandoned if they are no longer considered to be "meaningful." Second, nobody has the right to "impose" any of these teachings on anybody else, just as nobody has the right to impose his personal picture of Smith on anybody else.

It should be noted that the position taken by the dissenters does give us a certain freedom, but only if we are prepared to sacrifice another kind of freedom. We are free to make whatever drawing of Smith we desire, but only because we have lost the freedom to know Smith as he actually is. If we did have the freedom to know Smith as he is, then we would no longer have the freedom to alter Smith's picture at will. Similarly, if (as the official Church and orthodox Catholics believe) God has given us the freedom to know Him as He is, then we do not have the freedom to reject whatever doctrines we wish. If (as the dissenters believe) we have the freedom to reject any doctrines that are not "helpful" or "meaningful" to us, then this freedom is possible only because we do not have the freedom to know whether such teachings about God are in fact true.

It is important to keep this truth in mind because in their never-ending public relations campaign for dissent, those who reject Catholic doctrine have been most successful in creating the impression that they stand for freedom while orthodox Catholics are against it. In reality, each side in the controversy is defending freedom, but a different kind of freedom. The freedom of the dissenters is a secondary kind of freedom. Catholics loyal to Church doctrine are protecting the first and most important type of freedom—the freedom to know God truly.

Feeling in Place of Truth

If many dissenters reject doctrine, then what do they consider important for a Christian? Usually it is an inner feeling, a religious emotion, if you will. If a person has that inner feeling (which some dissenters refer to as a "religious experience"), then it does not matter what he or she may believe intellectually. You are a follower of Christ if you want to consider yourself one. Or you are a Christian if reading about Jesus in the Bible arouses a religious emotion in you, even if you believe that most of what you are reading is not actually true (for example, even if you reject the idea that Jesus is God or that He rose from the dead or that He had a special relationship with His Father). In short, the dissenters believe you can be a Christian and still regard what is written about Christ in the Bible as a myth or a fable that did not really occur. So long as you can find something of value in the "Christian fable," something that is helpful to you in your life, then you are a "Christian," even if you reject what the Bible itself presents as Christ's central message.

The "religious feeling" emphasized by many dissenters is quite similar to the "romantic feeling" that is stressed in some of our popular songs. In such songs, "love" is often described as an overpowering feeling. According to the songs, this overpowering feeling can come or go in a moment. It can cause you to "fall in love" with a total stranger. The love songs assure you that when the feeling comes upon you, it is more important than anything else.

For example, one well-known song contains this line: "How can it be wrong if it feels so right?" Another famous song speaks of seeing a "stranger across a crowded room" and knowing immediately that one is deeply in love with the stranger. Notice that what both songs are saying is that the only important thing is the feeling you have within and not the outside reality.

On the subject, "How can it be wrong if it feels so right," suppose, for example, that you are married. On your wedding day, you promised that you would always be faithful to your husband or wife. Since that day, you have been living up to your promise. But now you see a "stranger" and suddenly fall "head over heels in love." Perhaps over the years there have been some disputes between you and your marriage partner. Even if this is not the case, even if things are still going quite well in your marriage, the blunt truth is that you do not now experience a romantic feeling for your marriage partner that is quite as overpowering as the feeling you presently have towards a person you have just met.

Should you resist this passionate feeling or surrender to it? If you believe that the immediate experience is the only important reality, i. e., if you follow the advice of the love songs, then you may well conclude: "How can this be wrong if it feels so right." You may decide that no "rules" made in the past can bind you, nor can you be bound by any promise or commitment that you yourself made in the past to another person. Such a promise was only binding for the period when you were experiencing the overpowering feeling of love toward your husband or wife. Now that the feeling of love is being directed toward somebody else, you must be free to follow it and what you do cannot be declared wrong simply because of an abstract rule or promise.

Of course, following your feelings wherever they lead can often bring about consequences that affect other people. What happens to your three small children if you elope with the "stranger?" For that reason, the dissenters sometimes modify the principle that people should follow their feelings by saying that people should be able to do whatever feels right as long as it does not clearly hurt somebody else. With a little ingenuity it is usually possible to find a way in which there will be no clear harm to others, or at least to rationalize and pretend that such a way has been found. The three young children won't really be hurt, will they? After all, they're not losing a parent, they're actually gaining a "new aunt" or "uncle." Now they'll have two homes instead of one. Furthermore, whatever makes the parents satisfied and happy is bound to be beneficial to their children in the long run. Thus, if things can be "fixed" so that the consequences of the action will not hurt somebody else, then one is morally free to follow the overpowering feeling wherever it may lead.

Abortion

The controversy over the morality of abortion gives us another example of the great difference between basing moral judgments on an outside reality and basing them on an internal feeling. Why do the Catholic Church and other supporters of the Right to Life movement oppose abortion? It is because of the convictions that all human life is sacred, and that the unborn baby is an individual human life. This second conviction, which is certainly confirmed by the findings of modern biology, amounts to saying that the rightness or wrongness of abortion must be determined by a reality that exists outside of anybody's feelings—the reality of what an unborn child actually is. If the unborn baby is a human life, then no inner feeling can ever justify the killing of that baby.

As opposed to this conviction of the Catholic Church, however, consider the arguments of those who justify abortion (including, sad to say, a number of so-called "Catholic theologians"). If you look closely at their writings, you will see that they usually pay no attention whatever to the reality that exists outside of anybody's feelings. Those who justify abortion are simply not interested in discussing whether an unborn baby is in fact an individual human life. Instead, they argue that the rightness or wrongness of abortion depends solely upon the feelings of the woman involved. If the woman feels that what is within her has value, then it does. If the woman feels that what is within her does not have value, then it does not. Whatever she feels, the woman should have complete freedom to act in support of her feelings and nobody else should interfere. Any reality outside of feelings is simply irrelevant.

I experienced such an attitude first-hand when I had a discussion recently with a supporter of abortion. I asked him two questions: (1) Suppose that Mrs. Jones and Mrs. Smith are both carrying babies of exactly the same age. However, Mrs. Jones gives birth a few weeks prematurely. After birth, would you allow Mrs. Jones to take the life of her baby if she considered it desirable? If not, then why do you allow Mrs. Smith to take the life of the baby that is still within her, a baby of exactly the same age and development as the Jones baby?

(2) In general, the press and television refuse to use the phrase "unborn baby" in reporting about abortion. When questioned about this, representatives of the media have responded that they avoid the phrase because it is a matter of personal opinion whether what is within the mother should be described as an "unborn baby." Yet these same newspaper and television reporters repeatedly use the phrase "unborn baby" in discussing the campaign of the March of Dimes against birth defects. Isn't this an inconsistency? If what is within the mother is an unborn baby, then the term should be used in referring to the victims of abortion. If what is within the mother is not an unborn baby, then the term should not be used in talking about the March of Dimes campaign. Does not fair reporting require such consistency?

To these two questions, I received basically the same response from the pro-abortion advocate. In both cases, the answer was: "It depends upon how you feel."

With respect to the first question, the supporter of abortion said that he would not "feel right" in allowing a woman to kill her baby after birth. However, he did not have the same "feeling" about the baby before birth. He went on to speculate that there were probably two reasons for this difference in his feelings. First, you can see and hear a baby after birth, whereas you cannot see and hear a baby before birth. Second, a baby is usually given a name shortly after birth while a baby has no name before birth. In the words of the abortion supporter: "Once you see the baby face to face, once you hear the baby cry or touch the baby, once you call the baby by name, then it is only natural that you will have a very different feeling toward the baby."

In other words, it is the "friendly feeling" that gives value to the life of babies and not any reality that the babies themselves possess. After all, seeing and hearing and naming a baby do not change the reality of what the baby actually is. What they do change, however, is the emotion that we ourselves may have toward the baby. Under such logic, it would presumably be acceptable at some future date to kill babies after birth if by that time most people no longer experienced a "friendly feeling" just by looking at babies.

With respect to my second question, the response by the pro-abortionist was similar. No, he did not think that the media were inconsistent in using the phrase "unborn baby" with regard to a campaign against birth defects but refusing to use it with regard to abortion. Why? For this reason.

> When you are talking about the March of Dimes campaign against birth defects, you are speaking of a situation in which the woman wants her baby. She looks upon what is within her as her child. In such a circumstance, it is appropriate to use the term 'unborn baby.' However, when you are talking about abortion, you are speaking of a situation in which the woman does not want the baby and does not look upon what is within her as her child. This is a very different circumstance from the other. Here it is definitely not appropriate to use the phrase 'unborn baby'.

In summary, the unborn child is a baby if you want it to be a baby. If you wish otherwise, then it is not a baby. The mind can create whatever reality it desires and nothing need be regarded as true if it goes against your desires.

Such thinking is not confined to the one pro-abortion advocate with which I spoke. To the contrary, this mindset has attained great influence in our society, and people who are supposed to be intelligent continue to proclaim their allegiance to this mentality. As an example, I attended a debate on abortion between a pro-life doctor and a pro-abortion doctor in which the discussion was quite similar to the one I myself experienced. The "expert" pro-abortion doctor insisted that abortion did not involve the destruction of human life. Why? "Because, in order to be human, you have to be involved in a loving relationship with at least one other human being. Since the aborted fetus is not so involved, it is not human." The pro-life doctor immediately challenged this view by asking a question: "What about a baby who is born but then abandoned? Is such a baby also not human?" Without blinking an eye, the pro-abortion doctor replied: "It depends. If the abandoned baby cries out, and if someone responds to the cry, then it is human. However, if the abandoned baby cries out, and if nobody responds, then it is not human because it lacks any kind of loving relationship with another human being."

There's a line in a popular song that goes: "You're nobody until somebody loves you.'' Unfortunately, some of those who believe that immediate feeling is everything apply this statement literally.

At first glance, the question "Is abortion right or wrong?" seems to have nothing in common with the question "Can you actually fall in love with a stranger across a crowded room?" However, there is at least one similarity. Those who justify abortion are saying: "It does not matter what an unborn baby may be in reality. All that matters is how you feel toward the baby." Those who believe it is possible to fall deeply in love with a stranger are saying: "It does not matter what the stranger may be in reality. All that matters is how you feel toward the stranger."

By definition, a stranger is somebody you do not know. Can you really have a personal love for somebody that you do not know at all? Those who believe that love is solely an inner feeling will say "yes." Those who believe that love necessarily involves a relationship with an outside reality will say "no," and will respond as follows:

You can certainly have a strong sensual attraction toward a stranger you see across a crowded room, just as you can have a sensual attraction toward a picture in a book. That is something purely physical although, even in this situation, you must first see the stranger with your eyes (and thus have sense knowledge) before you can have a sense attraction. However, a human person is far more than a physical body and, for that reason, a truly human love involves far more than a sensual attraction. For two persons to love in a truly human way, they must know and relate to each other on a number of levels (intellectually and spiritually, as well as physically), and such a relationship is not possible with a person who is a total stranger. While sensual attraction can be the emotion that first makes one person interested in knowing another, it is only the first step. This physical feeling can be present even in situations when there is no true human love between the persons. Conversely, a deep human love can exist between two persons when there has never been a strong sensual attraction (as in the case of brothers) or when such a powerful feeling once was present but is not any longer (as in the case of many married couples). So the argument goes.

Is God a Total Stranger?

As we have seen, the basic problem that many dissenters have with Church doctrine is their underlying belief that we can know little or nothing about God as He actually is. In their view, even the Bible is not so much the "Word of God" (that is, God revealing Himself to man) as it is the "word of man" (that is, a record of what human beings in past ages imagined God to be). Since they consider it to be the "word of man," dissenters hold that there can be many mistakes in the Bible. Therefore, the men and women of today are free to discard anything in the Bible that they judge to be no longer meaningful.

This is true even with respect to the words and deeds of Jesus Christ Himself. For example, many dissenters will tell you bluntly that they do not believe that the miracles attributed to Our Lord in the New Testament actually took place. Nor were the sayings of Our Lord really uttered by Him. According to these dissenters, both the words and deeds of Jesus were actually created by the early Christians some time after the death of Christ. In other words, we do not know and cannot know "the historical Christ"—the Jesus who actually existed. All that we can know is the "biblical Christ"—the way that the early Christians felt about Jesus.

Needless to say, the official teaching of the Catholic Church strongly rejects this view. In fact, *the Bible itself* strongly rejects such a position. Like the person who insists that the rightness or wrongness of abortion depends upon what an unborn baby actually is (and not our feelings); like the person who believes that you cannot have true love for another person unless you also have true knowledge; the Church and the Bible both teach that we most certainly can know Jesus as He actually was and is. Both Church and Bible emphasize that the biblical Christ *is* the historical Christ. Yes, the early Christians "felt" a certain way about Jesus, but they felt that way because it was something true that many of them had personally witnessed and not because it was something that they themselves had made up.

In contrast with the Church and the Bible, many dissenters are like the person who believes that the value of an unborn baby does not depend upon the baby itself but upon the way that others feel about the baby. Therefore, while beliefs such as the Resurrection of Jesus or His Real Presence in the Eucharist may be important, they are only important because people find them "meaningful." They are not important because of any element of literal truth they may contain. In fact, they may *not* be literally true at all. Perhaps, suggest the dissenters, such beliefs are "purely symbolic."

What do the dissenters mean by "purely symbolic?" As applied to the Eucharist, it means that Catholics do not receive the actual Body and Blood of Jesus in Holy Communion. Instead, the Eucharist is similar to a ring that a husband gives to his wife when he must go away for a time. The ring is not the husband. In itself, the ring is no different from a hundred other rings. Nevertheless, the ring has a very important "symbolic value," but only because the husband and wife have agreed to give the ring a value that it does not itself possess. The value comes solely from their feelings, and they can withdraw this value from the ring whenever they wish.

As applied to the Resurrection of Jesus, the phrase "purely symbolic" means that Jesus did not literally rise from the dead. Christians can say that "the Spirit of Jesus is alive today" in the same way that Americans can say "the spirit of Abraham Lincoln is alive today." Neither Jesus nor Lincoln is literally present, but they have important "symbolic value" for us today—Lincoln as a patriotic symbol and Jesus as a religious symbol. In that sense, they are "alive." In that sense, they are "risen" and not "dead."

Does the Actual Truth Really Matter?

What about the claim of the dissenters that it does not really matter whether beliefs such as the Resurrection or the Real Presence are literally true? In response, it might be said that it certainly matters to the Church, to the inspired writers of the Bible, and to orthodox Catholics.

In pretending that the literal truth of Church doctrine is not nearly so important as the symbolic value, the dissenters appear to be engaged in something that is as old as Aesop's Fables. Do you remember the fable about the fox ands the grapes? Because the fox could not reach the grapes, he managed to convince himself that he did not really want them. Similarly, the dissenters, believing that men cannot know the real truth about Christ, try to convince both themselves and others that the "symbolic value" of Christ is all that really matters.

Well, it is not all that really matters. To use the example presented previously, a wife will cherish highly the ring given to her by her husband. Nevertheless, she is well aware that the "symbolic presence" of her husband through the ring is not the same as the "real presence" of her husband. If she were told that her husband was "present" in the next room, she would be very disappointed if she walked into that room and found only the ring. She would never say to herself: "You know, it doesn't actually matter if my husband is here or not, so long as I have the ring to make me feel good."

Just as there is all the difference in the world between a "symbolic presence" of the husband through his ring and his "real presence," so there is a tremendous difference between a "symbolic presence" of Our Lord in the Eucharist and a "Real Presence," or between a "symbolic" Resurrection of Jesus and a real Resurrection. For that reason, both the Church and the Bible have gone to great lengths to emphasize that such doctrines are literally true.

As one example, consider how Sacred Scripture goes out of its way to stress that the Resurrection of Jesus is a real and physical Resurrection, and not simply a "symbolic" Resurrection. Here is the account in St. Luke's Gospel of the appearance of the Risen Christ to His apostles:

> Jesus Himself stood in their midst and said to them, "Peace to you." In their panic and fright they thought they were seeing a ghost. He said to them, "Why are you disturbed? Why do such ideas cross your mind? Look at my hands and my feet; it is really I. Touch me, and see that a ghost does not have flesh and bones as I do." As he said this he showed them his hands and feet. They were still incredulous for sheer joy and wonder, so he said to them, "Have you anything here to eat?" They gave him a piece of cooked fish, which he took and ate in their presence. Then he said to them, "Recall those words I spoke to you when I was still with you: everything written about me in the law of Moses and the prophets and psalms had to be fulfilled." Then he opened their minds to the understanding of the Scriptures.
>
> He said to them: "Thus it is written that the Messiah must suffer and rise from the dead on the third day. In his name, penance for the remission of sins is to be preached to all the nations, beginning at Jerusalem. You are witnesses of all this." (Luke 24:36-48)

Jesus is well aware that some will try to explain away his Resurrection as only a "symbolic" happening. Therefore, He tells His Apostles directly: "Look at my hands and my feet; it is really I. Touch me, and see that a ghost does not have flesh and bones as I do." Then, to demonstrate the point further, Our Lord eats a piece of cooked fish.

St. John's Gospel tells us that Thomas was not present when Jesus first appeared to His Apostles. A week later, however, Thomas was present and Jesus proved to the doubting Thomas that His Resurrection was a real and physical event. He did this by having Thomas examine and even touch the wounds in Our Lord's hands and side.

In summary, the Bible considers it of the utmost importance that every follower of Christ understand clearly that the Resurrection of Jesus is literally true. As St. Paul writes in another book of the Bible (I Corinthians 15): "If Christ has not been raised, our preaching is void of content and your faith is empty too. Indeed, we should then be exposed as false witnesses of God, for we have borne witness before him that he raised up Christ. . . . If our hopes in Christ are limited to this life only, we are the most pitiable of men. But as it is, Christ is now raised from the dead, the first fruits of those who have fallen asleep."

Before leaving this topic, it might be good to point out that there is a sense in which it is proper to use the word "symbol" in connection with Church doctrine. As we discussed in the first book, it often happens that a word will have several meanings, meanings that can be related to each other but are also different in some respect. A favorite trick of Church dissenters is to confuse orthodox Catholics by taking words with more than one meaning (e.g., "infallibility" or "authority") and using them in a manner different from the sense in which they are employed by the Church.

In today's usage, the word "symbol" commonly refers to something that represents another reality but is not in itself what it represents. Thus, a ring represents the husband but is not in itself the husband. In this sense of the word, (the sense used by dissenters in speaking of Christian doctrine), the "symbol" can never be the actual reality.

However, there is another meaning of the word. "Symbol" can refer to something that has both an outer aspect and an inner aspect. In that sense of the word, what happens outside is a "symbol" of what is actually happening inside. Thus, a frown or a smile are "symbols" or "signs" of the way a person feels within. In the same way, the sacrament of Baptism is a "symbol" or "sign" because the pouring of water on the head of the person baptized represents what is truly happening within, i.e., the coming of God's grace to the soul, and the cleansing from original sin.

The difference between these two meanings of "symbol" is important. In the first meaning, a "symbol" is *not really* what it represents. In the second meaning, a "symbol" is *really* what it represents because it is the outer aspect of a reality that is actually taking place within. In this second sense of the word, the Church sometimes refers to the visible aspects of the Catholic religion (e.g., the sacraments) as "symbols of the faith."

To avoid this problem with words, we have been using the phrase "purely symbolic" to describe the position of the dissenters with respect to Christian doctrine. Nevertheless, orthodox Catholics should be aware of the two different meanings of "symbol" in case the dissenters attempt to create confusion on this matter.

Why the Dissenters May Not Be Recognized

Having tried to present the general view of the dissenters as clearly as possible, let us consider one additional problem. Sometimes those who are in fact dissenters are not recognized as such by other Catholics. Why is this the case?

We have already presented one reason in a previous chapter, namely, that the dissenters can disagree among themselves. Some reject only a few Church doctrines, while others reject almost everything. If you happen to be talking to a dissenter about a Church teaching that he continues to hold, he may strongly affirm his faith in that doctrine and criticize those who dissent from it. In such a situation, it is easy to believe that he is an opponent of the dissenters, rather than a dissenter himself. Such an impression is likely to continue, unless your conversation goes into those areas where the person to whom you are talking is himself a dissenter. Only then will it become clear that he believes in the basic principle of dissent, i. e., the principle that Catholics can choose for themselves which Church doctrines to believe and which to deny.

In addition to the internal disagreements among the dissenters themselves, there are two other reasons that some Church dissenters are not recognized as such:

Reason One: The dissenters often employ the same language as orthodox Catholics.

Reason Two: The dissenters can do many good things. Seeing their good qualities, people find it hard to believe that these individuals are dissenters and especially if the dissenters are the "inside" kind who achieve their goal not by denying Church doctrine openly but by avoiding all mention of it (or minimizing it as far as possible) in their presentations.

Let us consider each of these explanations in turn.

1. Often the dissenters employ the *same language* as orthodox Catholics. As a result, certain views can appear on the surface to be acceptable even though they are actually very much opposed to Christian doctrine.

We have considered already a number of instances where the dissenters deliberately create this confusion. Even when this is not the case, however, confusion can easily result. The basic reason is that it is natural for both the dissenters and orthodox Catholics to use similar language in describing their religious feelings.

To illustrate this by an example presented earlier in this chapter, we know there is a world of difference between a man and woman who are truly in love and a man and woman who have only a strong physical attraction or emotional feeling toward each other. Nevertheless, despite the fact that one couple is truly in love and the other is not, both couples will use the same language in describing their feelings, the language of romantic love. There is a good reason for this. On the level of feeling, both couples are experiencing much the same thing. The difference is that the couple truly in love has something *more* than feeling, while the couple not truly in love has *only* feeling. An outsider, hearing the same expressions of romantic love from both couples, will have great difficulty in deciding which couple is truly in love and which is not. This will only become evident at a later time, perhaps when the strong feeling is no longer present or when the man and woman must make sacrifices to preserve their relationship. Then, and only then, will it be clear which couple is motivated by something more than feeling.

As both couples use the same language of romantic love, so dissenters and orthodox Catholics frequently use the same language to express their religious feelings. Thus, the dissenters will talk of "Christian love," or of an "encounter with Christ," or of a "commitment to the Lord," or even of the value of the Mass and the Eucharist. Orthodox Catholics employ the same language. The difference between orthodox Catholics and dissenters is not their feelings, which may well be similar. The difference is that orthodox Cahtolics believe in something *more* than feeling, while many dissenters are guided *only* by their inner feeling. For instance, both dissenters and orthodox Catholics believe that the Eucharist has value. For orthodox Catholics, however, the primary value of the Eucharist is determined by what the Sacrament actually is—the Body and Blood of Jesus. For dissenters, the primary value of the Eucharist is determined not by what the Eucharist is in reality but (like the husband's ring) by what it "symbolizes" to men in their religious feelings.

As with the married couples, it may be difficult to spot the very real difference between dissenters and orthodox Catholics, except in those situations where a Christian doctrine requires people to sacrifice or to go against their inner feelings. In such situations the dissenters, believing that inner religious feeling is primary, will reject the doctrine as "outdated" or "no longer meaningful for modern man." In contrast, orthodox Catholics will tend to assume that it is not the doctrine but their feelings that need to be revised.

Outside of this case, a dissenter can often appear to be orthodox. As one example, I recently attended a lecture on Christ by a prominent "liberal" theologian. His presentation appeared to be not only acceptable but quite effective until he was asked the following question: "Suppose that someday a group of scientists found the actual grave where Jesus was buried. As you view the Resurrection, would it or would it not be possible that the bodily remains of Jesus Christ might still be in that grave?" He replied: "Based upon our modern understanding of the Resurrection, this would be possible."

It was only this specific question which made it clear that the "learned" theologian's "modern understanding" of the Resurrection was actually a position so old that it was rejected explicitly by the Bible. If the clarifying question had not been asked, or if the dissenter had answered in an ambiguous way, many people would have departed from the lecture-hall without realizing that the speaker they naturally assumed to be orthodox was in fact a person who denied the Resurrection as a real event and believed in it only in a purely symbolic fashion.

2. In addition to language, a second reason that Church dissenters may go unrecognized is that they can *do many good things*. Observing their good actions, many Catholics will find it difficult to believe that these individuals are dissenters. How can the dissenters do much that is good while still undermining Church doctrine? To answer that question, let us start with the observation of a clergyman who spent his life studying the conflicts that have taken place in the Church throughout history. With regard to such religious disputes, the clergyman commented that it often seemed to be the case that people were right in what they affirmed but wrong in what they denied. They were right in what they emphasized but wrong in what they overlooked. They were right in what they were *for* but wrong in what they were *against*.

Applying this to the dissenters, let us give a brief description of their way of thinking and then separate what they affirm from what they deny or ignore.[1]

The dissenters approach Christ and His Church from the viewpoint of man. They are concerned with human feelings and emotions. Therefore, they emphasize the concrete and personal character of human existence, i.e., man's changing states of consciousness, his desires and fears, and his constant need to make personal decisions.

While considering Christ from the viewpoint of man, the dissenters are usually not interested in presenting a systematic elaboration of religious truth (Catholic doctrine). Hence they by-pass, or give scant attention to, such questions as the nature of God as He is in Himself (something that many dissenters believe to be unknowable) or to God as the Creator and Governor of the universe. Instead, the dissenters center their attention on the "meaning" God has for man. How do God and the Church have meaning for men and women in their day-to-day existence? How do God and the Church help men and women to meet their problems, overcome the obstacles and make the right decisions in their daily lives?

Finally, the dissenters tend to emphasize action rather than thought. Remember that many dissenters believe that we cannot know things as they are in themselves. Therefore thought, which deals with knowledge, is less important than action, which involves a personal response to the immediate situation. Thus, the dissenters stress the concern that Christians should have for everything human, the necessity of Church involvement in man's struggle for a good life, the importance of working for a better world here on earth. They do not stress either Catholic doctrine or general principles of morality, because both doctrine and rules of morality involve thought and, in the view of the dissenters, we can never be sure of the truth of these thoughts. They say that we can never be certain whether Christ is God, so this doctrine does not matter. We can never be certain whether abortion is always wrong, so this general rule of morality does not matter. All that matters is the immediate situation and our feelings and actions in that situation. Does Christ (whether God or not) arouse in us today a religious feeling that leads us to work for a better world? Does the life within the pregnant woman (whether a human baby or not) arouse in her a maternal feeling that makes her willing to be a mother?

Since the dissenters regard Catholic doctrine and general rules of morality as uncertain, the teaching of the Pope naturally falls into the same category. Instead of obeying the moral and doctrinal statements of Church authorities, the dissenters urge Catholics to make such decisions themselves.

Employing this brief summary, let us now separate what the dissenters affirm and emphasize from what they deny or ignore.

Dissenters Affirm and Emphasize: The importance of responding to human feelings, to the emotions, desires, and fears of people, the importance of the immediate situation, the importance of personal decision-making, of taking the initiative yourself, the importance of applying your religion in a concrete way to the conditions in which you live, the importance of social-action programs to help other people.

Dissenters Deny or Ignore: The importance of any area outside of human feeling, the importance of knowing God as He is in Himself, the importance of the religious truth taught by Christ and entrusted to His Church to be passed on unchanged to all generations, the importance of general moral rules that go beyond the feeling of the moment, the importance of obeying the Pope acting in his capacity as the Vicar of Christ when he makes a decision on a matter of faith or morals. Once we have made this separation, we can see immediately that the problem lies with what the dissenters deny or ignore. With respect to these matters, the Church tells the dissenters that they are wrong, and seriously so. It is very good to respond to human feeling, but we must go beyond that. By God's own invitation, we have been called to know Him as He is. God has revealed Himself to us in the Old and New Testament. This Revelation was confided by Jesus Christ to His Church, a visible body with an organized structure. Faith is a response of the mind by which, through God's grace, we accept the truths that God has revealed. However, faith must not be sterile but must flow out in acts of love for God and for our fellow men. Living this life of faith, hope, and love, with which we are endowed at Baptism, we grow ever more like to Christ. When life is done, the light of Faith will blossom into the light of Glory and, possessing God by knowledge and love in the Beatific Vision, we will share God's happiness with all the members of Christ's Mystical Body throughout eternity.

Neglected Truths

The Church believes that it is vital for Catholics to stress the values that the dissenters neglect. At the same time, however, there is no problem with what the dissenters affirm. Far from contradicting Church teaching, the insights emphasized by the dissenters can be of great help, provided that (unlike the dissenters) we also affirm the literal truth and importance of Catholic doctrine.

Thus, the dissenters focus on the value of personal initiative in daily life. They dismiss the value of Church authority. Yet is it possible to stress *both* the value of Church authority in presenting us with Christ's teaching *and* the value of personal initiative in carrying out this teaching of Christ in our daily life? There is no necessary contradiction between Church authority and personal initiative (assuming, of course, that the personal initiative is not being used *against* Christ's teaching.)

Similarly, there should be no opposition between social action and Church doctrine. To the contrary, one of the most important Church doctrines is the belief that the test of our love for God is the love we show for our neighbor and particularly those people who are in need. According to both the Bible and the Church, not only must we love our neighbor as ourselves, but we must go even farther and see Christ Himself in our neighbor. While the dissenters may have created an opposition in their own minds between social action and Church doctrine, it is not only possible to concentrate on both but God's will that we do so.

While the dissenters deny or neglect aspects of Catholicism that are absolutely essential, it is still possible for orthodox Catholics to learn much from the elements that the dissenters stress. For instance, as we have discussed throughout this book, most loyal Catholics are not personally working as hard to promote orthodox doctrine as the dissenters are to promote their challenge to orthodox doctrine. That is a key reason the dissenters often seem to be winning, and the explanation appears to lie in the fact that the dissenters have been stressing the importance of "grass-roots" personal activity in a way that orthodox Catholics have not. Ironically, the efforts of the dissenters can provide orthodox Catholics with a lesson that will make us much more effective in defending the Pope and supporting Church teaching.

However, to return to the major theme of this section, it should now be clear why some dissenters are not easily recognized as such either by their bishop or by many loyal Catholics in their parishes. Instead of attacking Church doctrine directly, these dissenters simply omit it. At first glance their speeches and writings appear to be excellent. So do the religious education programs that they devise for their parishes. Their programs stress the importance of social action. They emphasize the value of religious feeling. They talk about the fears and desires of men and women and about the problems that people face in the world. It is only upon close study that it becomes clear that there is one thing these programs neglect. While they concentrate on many other aspects, they consistently fail to emphasize or even mention that the doctrinal teaching of the Church is literally (not just symbolically) true and that this doctrinal teaching is of utmost importance to our Christian life.

And, if loyal Catholics attempt to remedy this defect by asking for books and programs that stress *both* social action *and* doctrine, most dissenters adamantly refuse. At times they become so angry at these requests that one suspects they must have developed a kind of "allergy" to any attempt to emphasize orthodox Catholic doctrine. For some reason, and despite their "good qualities," the dissenters are determined to do everything in their power both to avoid doctrinal emphasis themselves, and to prevent others from reaching the Catholic people with strongly orthodox programs that promote the Church's official teaching.

NOTES

[1] A paperback book that I have found quite helpful in preparing this section is *Keeping Your Balance in the Modern Church* by Rev. Hugh O'Connell, C.SS.R. (Liguorian Pamphlets, 1968). Unfortunately, this book is currently out of print.

7.
How Did The Dissenters
Get That Way?

We have considered the ideas of the dissenters and their "intellectual assumptions." When we look at the chaos they have created, however, it is hard to avoid raising another question relative to the dissenters, not about their views, but about their character. How did the dissenters develop as they did? As we have just seen, it would be a mistake to assume that they were all bad. To the contrary, many dissenters started out with the best of motives.

Students of literature are familiar with the concept of the "tragic hero." In fiction, the "tragic hero" is a person who has many fine attributes but who fails because of one serious flaw that destroys everything else. If we consider the dissenters, we see such a flaw, a defect that we can observe clearly in them, and also a defect that we who want to promote Church teaching must always guard against in ourselves. The flaw is *pride*. The dissenters believe they know more than others, that they have an insight into the Christian religion that neither the Pope nor "average" Catholics possess.

It is perhaps understandable that the dissenters would be tempted in this way. In fact, many of them are quite intelligent. Nevertheless, Our Lord Himself tells us that, if we are truly to understand Him, we must always be child-like in our attitudes. As we begin to think that we know more than everybody else, we get farther and farther away from Christ rather than closer to Him.

We have used the word "pride" to describe this flaw in the dissenters. But perhaps an even better phrase to sum up what happened to them is "loss of reverence." Before they became dissenters—before they "knew so much"—most dissenters had a reverence for the authority of the Pope and for Church teaching, a reverence they have now lost. Let us look, therefore, at the idea of "reverence" and how easily one can lose it.

Reverence

There is a paradox that we express in many of our popular sayings. Consider, for instance the following statements:

    a. Familiarity breeds contempt.
    b. No man is a hero to his valet.
    c. You can't see the forest for the trees.
    d. A cynic is one who knows the price of everything and the value
       of nothing.

What do all these sayings have in common? What they tell us is that, ironic as it might seem at first, one can miss the full picture by getting too close. Because we see all the details (the trees) we can fail to see what the details add up to (the forest). The more "familiar" we become (like a valet), the easier it is to lose reverence and to hold in contempt what we once treasured.

C. S. Lewis, commenting on what would happen when man first set foot on the moon, wrote that at the moment this event occurred, men would possess the moon for science but lose it forever for poetry. In other words, once we could measure it, once we could walk on it, the moon would become "just another object" and would no longer arouse in us a feeling of awe.

Children can have a similar difficulty in retaining reverence for their parents. At an early age they usually hold their parents in awe. But then, often during the teenage years, the awe can easily turn to contempt. Part of this may be the pressure of growing up. Another aspect, however, is that as they grow older, they know more details about their parents, see more and more of the human side of their mother and father. They even find that they can do some things better than their parents. At this stage it is very, very easy to lose reverence.

Our Lord Himself put this paradox best. We read the following in the 13th Chapter of St. Matthew:

> When Jesus had finished these parables He left the district; and, coming to His home town, He taught the people in their synagogue in such

a way that they were astonished and said, "Where did the man get this wisdom and miraculous powers? This is the carpenter's son surely? Is not his mother the woman called Mary, and his brothers James and Joseph and Simon and Jude? His sisters, too, are they not all here with us, so where did the man get it all." And they would not accept him. But Jesus said to them, "A prophet is only despised in his own country and his own house" and He did not work many miracles there because of their lack of faith.

Jesus Himself experienced a lack of reverence from His own neighbors. Why? Because they knew so many details about Him. They knew His background. They knew Mary. They knew Joseph. They knew His relatives described here as His "brothers" and "sisters." Because they knew all these facts, they missed the most important reality of all. Their very "familiarity" kept them from understanding, kept them from reverence.

As an aside, I know that some dedicated Catholics occasionally wish that we were back at the time of Our Lord so that we could see Him personally. Perhaps it is better that we are not. If we had been His neighbors, would we too have failed to see the most important thing about Jesus?

The problem we have been describing is the one that affects the dissenters with respect to Church teaching. Like small children with their parents, they started out with reverence toward Catholic doctrine, but then they became more and more knowledgeable about little details. As the neighbors of Jesus knew a thousand small things about His background, so the dissenters came to know a thousand small things about the human elements in the Church, items such as the personalities of the various Popes or how a particular Church council featured a controversy between Bishop X and Bishop Y over the meaning of an important Church teaching. Add a thousand other details and soon the dissenters could no longer see the forest for the trees. They lost reverence for the very Church doctrines they had originally hoped to defend.

In the debate between theological dissenters and "ordinary" Catholics who remain loyal to Church teaching, those who wish to defend the Pope often lack this extensive knowledge of details. What results in such discussions is similar to a debate that might be imagined between one of Our Lord's next-door neighbors and someone who reverenced Him. The neighbor knows endless bits of information. He can tell you when Our Lord gets up in the morning, even what He has for breakfast. The committed Christian knows none of this, and for that reason, the neighbor can often make the committed Christian look uninformed during their "debate."

But the truth is that such details, while interesting, are basically insignificant. Furthermore, it is far better not to know these facts if it causes one to lose the most important part of the picture.

Of course, familiarity does not inevitably lead to contempt. Our Lady is the best example. She knew Christ better than anyone, yet her knowledge only led to deeper reverence. Nevertheless, the more facts we know, the greater the temptation can be to glory in our knowledge of detail and laud it over those who do not have such information. In order to be like Our Lady, we must constantly humble ourselves. Then, we too can be "familiar with all the details" while still retaining those child-like qualities that Our Lord spoke of as necessary for His followers.

In order to be as effective as possible in defending Church doctrine, loyal Catholics must try to match the dissenters in their knowledge of details. Otherwise the dissenters can make the defenders of the Pope look foolish. But at this point, when loyal Catholics do become so familiar, there can be the danger that we also will lose reverence and begin to put ourselves in the place of the Lord, the very mistake that so tragically ruined the activity of the dissenters. Even as we go forth to defend Church teaching, therefore, let us pray unceasingly to Our Blessed Lady who is the Model of Familiarity with Reverence.

8.
Why Do The Bishops Appear To Do Nothing About Dissent?

> The bishops, who obtained many powers for themselves at the Council, are often to blame because in this crisis they are not exercising their powers as they should. . . . If all the bishops would deal decisively with these aberrations as they occur, the situation would be different.
>
> —*Cardinal Seper*

In a preceding chapter we discussed the fact that local bishops (as well as other Church authorities) often appear to do nothing to check dissent, despite appeals for action from the Vatican. Let us now return to this subject and attempt to explain in a more extensive way the problems that today's bishops believe they face.

I do this because I believe it is most important for faithful Catholics to understand thoroughly the feelings of local Church authorities such as the bishops. There are two reasons such an awareness is crucial.

First, if loyal Catholics are not so aware, they will almost certainly become disillusioned and even bitter when, after realizing the devastating problems caused by dissent, they appeal to their bishop for help and get nothing in return. At that point a loyal Catholic may often feel like a person who has run into a stone wall. He is stunned at the apparent indifference, the total inactivity and, in some cases, the patronizing attitude of their bishops who are the very men he has been taught to revere, the very men who are supposed to be working unceasingly to promote Church doctrine.

If you know in advance that a stone wall lies ahead of you, you can possibly figure out a way around it, especially if you learn everything you can about the wall and study it very carefully. On the other hand, if you do not even suspect that the stone wall is there, you may run into it at full speed and be shattered by the result.

In addition to avoiding disillusionment and bitterness, there is a second reason for loyal Catholics to learn everything they can about the feelings of their bishops. The ultimate goal is to encourage your bishop to act effectively in support of Church teaching. But different bishops have different feelings. To encourage your bishop to act effectively, you must respond successfully to the personal feelings that he has. The reason that one bishop does not act against dissent can be quite different from the reason that another bishop does not act.

For instance, Bishop A may feel that he has little power to do anything. To overcome this problem, you must convince him of the opposite. In contrast, Bishop B knows that he has power but is fearful that any action by him could boomerang. Meanwhile, Bishop C has yet a third attitude. He thinks he is acting effectively but does not realize that his personal actions never get down to the local parish level.

In each case, the bishop has a different feeling. To obtain effective action, you must respond successfully to whatever is holding your bishop back. You will not achieve your goal if you respond to something else that is a problem for another bishop, but not for him. Thus, Bishops B and C do not have to be persuaded that they have the power to act. This is Bishop A's problem. Bishop C does not have to be persuaded that his actions will be helpful and not counterproductive. This is Bishop B's problem.

Since understanding the attitude of your bishop is such an important step in promoting orthodoxy, let us list as many reasons as possible that bishops may not at present be acting effectively in support of Church teaching. A good place to begin is to consider how the office of bishop has evolved in practice. What does the typical bishop do?

Father and Administrator

A bishop who heads a diocese (and some are either auxiliaries to the bishop who heads the diocese or function in some other capacity) is usually attempting to fulfill two important roles. First, the bishop is expected to act like a father. Second, the bishop is expected to act like the administrator of a large organization.

As a father, the bishop acts as a symbolic figure to many groups within the diocese. One of his principal functions is to appear at a great many ceremonies that are taking place within the diocese. The bishop's presence is a sign of encouragement to all the Catholic groups that are working within the Church. Depending upon the size of the diocese (there are, of course, both large dioceses and small dioceses), this ceremonial or fatherly function can take up a great amount of the bishop's time.

As an administrator, the task of the bishop is to try to keep a large organization operating smoothly. In a large diocese there may be hundreds of parishes, thousands of priests, additional thousands of religious, and perhaps as many as a million lay people. To keep this organization going requires the bishop to act like the chairman of the board of a big company. Many management decisions must be made. A great amount of time is spent on the financial and administrative aspects of the diocese.

Since the modern bishop acts both like a father and like an administrator, let us consider why a father might not act to stop dissent, and also why an administrator might not.

The Father

Imagine that a father is facing a serious problem with one of his children. Let us call the child "Jim." Jim has begun to rebel against his father's authority. He is doing certain things that disturb the father very much. To develop the example even further, let us suppose that Jim has begun to question and react against some of the values that his father believes are important, the values that the family had always practiced. For instance, Jim no longer goes to Mass. He has begun to drink frequently. Finally, Jim has found a girlfriend and, while remaining unmarried and continuing to dwell in his father's house, Jim has decided on a "live-in relationship" with his girl. Faced with these actions on the part of Jim, what should a father do? What would you do if you were in such a situation?

Most fathers would probably take one of two courses of action. The first course would be to stand up very strongly for the values that Jim is denying, to say to Jim, "If you can't practice these values, then get out of the house."

The late Bing Crosby said once that this was the kind of action he would take if any of his children ever attempted a live-in relation with a boyfriend or girlfriend. Many other fathers would agree with him. Such a response has the advantage of protecting the values that are so important. On the other hand, could this kind of firm action lead to an irrevocable break between parent and child? That is the reason some parents hesitate to act in this way.

They are afraid that if they tell Jim that he must either follow the traditional family values or get out of the house, the decision of Jim will be to get out of the house. In other words, they are convinced that strong action will make things worse. They will lose their children forever, and they do not want to lose their children. Is it not better, they ask themselves, to keep the lines of communication open?

Such parents are hoping desperately that time will be on their side. They avoid any strong action now in the hope that Jim will eventually grow out of his present hostile attitudes. "Perhaps things will get better in the long run." Unfortunately, instead of better, things may well get worse.

As there is a real danger that strong action by the father may cause Jim to leave the house forever, so there is another kind of real danger if the father avoids taking strong action. Even if the father says that he believes drunkenness and sexual relationships outside marriage are seriously wrong, his apparent tolerance of Jim's activity seems to give the opposite message. The surface unity with Jim is preserved, but at the cost of jeopardizing important values.

The Other Children in the Family

To complicate the matter, let us imagine that Jim is not the only child in the family. Suppose that he is the eldest son. There are several other children who continue to believe strongly in the values their father has taught them. What will be the effect on them of allowing Jim to drink and to carry on a "live-in" sexual relationship in the same house? Let us call these children Tom and Sue. Tom and Sue feel helpless to stop Jim's assault on the family values. Naturally enough, they presume that it is the father who should react. In order to defend the values that they hold dear, the values they have been taught, they begin to push the father to do something. To put it bluntly, they nag the father at every opportunity.

In this situation, an interesting thing can happen. Instead of standing up to Jim, the father may respond sharply to Tom and Sue. You see, Tom and Sue are questioning his administrative decision not to act. Jim, on the other hand, "simply" wants to do whatever he wishes. The very fact that the father himself may wonder whether his course of action is the right one can lead him to react even more sharply against Tom and Sue than he would if he had complete confidence in his own decision.

At any rate, the father responds by telling Tom and Sue to mind their own business. Or perhaps he responds by refusing to admit to Tom and Sue that there is a problem by pretending not to see what everybody really knows is happening. In either case, such a response frustrates Tom and Sue even more. They realize that the current family atmosphere is no longer supportive of the values in which they deeply believe.

Yet the only person (in their view) who can change things, either refuses to admit there is a problem or refuses to act. They may ask themselves: Why does my father speak up so strongly to me when he refuses to speak up to Jim?

With many fathers there is a simple reason for this double standard. They speak up strongly to Tom and Sue because they believe Tom and Sue will obey. In other words, there is no danger that strong words will cause Tom and Sue to leave the family. On the other hand, if they spoke up strongly to Jim, he would revolt and leave immediately.

While such an attitude is perhaps understandable, what it actually accomplishes is to punish Tom and Sue for their loyalty. Meanwhile, the person who is challenging the basic values of the family continues to act day by day in a way that weakens these convictions both for himself and for others. Yet, despite it all, the father continues to hope that "someday things will get better" and even to congratulate himself on the fact that his policy of avoiding strong action toward Jim has kept his eldest son in the family, at least in a nominal sense.

The attitude of the father towards Jim is precisely the attitude that many bishops have toward Church dissenters. The sharp reaction of the father to Tom and Sue when they attempt to push him into defending important values is precisely the attitude of many bishops towards Catholics who urge them to do something about the problem of dissent within the Church.

The Bishop as Administrator

Now let us consider the bishop as an administrator of a large organization. Administrators of large organizations have an instinctive tendency to place short-range practical considerations over long-range theoretical considerations. The basic reason for this tendency is that the administrator must concentrate on the day-to-day functioning of the organization.

Another way of putting this is that administrators are often tempted to obtain peace at almost any price. The one thing that disrupts the day-to-day functioning of an organization is conflict. As with the father, administrators tend to believe that, if only the problem can be avoided, it may cure itself.

According to Emerson, Napoleon once directed that all his letters should be left unopened for three weeks. Why? Well, Napoleon thought that by adopting this policy a large part of the correspondence would dispose of itself and would thus no longer require an answer.

That is a typical response of the administrator, i.e., to delay facing a crisis or to postpone action indefinitely, especially if it is foreseen that the action would bring on a major disruption. They say, "let us keep the peace today and perhaps things will improve tomorrow."

A second point to make both about the bishop and any head of a large organization is that the bigger the organization is the more the administrator must of necessity depend upon other people. In that situation, an administrator has to delegate great amounts of work. The larger the organization, the more there is a need for specialists in many particular areas. As a result, a condition soon develops in which the general administrator does not have the expertise to match that of his own specialists in the particular area in which they function. What this means is that the administrator often feels uncomfortable and unequipped to debate on any theoretical level with his own specialists. On the theoretical level, the administrator feels that his specialists know so many facts about their particular area that they could make him look ridiculous if he publicly challenged them on a matter within their field. Thus, he tries to avoid any such theoretical "disputes" with specialists within his own organization. Instead, the administrator concentrates on "practical" discussions, about the day-to-day functioning of the organization. This is subject-matter with which he is familiar and comfortable.

Because they are managers of large organizations, many bishops follow a policy similar to the one we have just described. The administrator-bishop himself concentrates on the practical decisions of his diocese) e.g., the raising of money and the allocation of personnel). Other matters are delegated to subordinates, even if the matters are very important (e.g., the teaching of Catholic doctrine). The subordinates are expected to become specialists in the fields for which they have been selected.

To illustrate how some bishops act toward their own specialists, let me give two examples involving bishops. I will call them Bishop Jones and Cardinal Smith. Both manage important American dioceses.

I know Bishop Jones personally. For that reason, I can assure you that his personal sympathies are all with the "traditional" Catholics. Bishop Jones wants to see doctrine stressed—orthodox Catholic doctrine. On an emotional level, Bishop Jones strongly supports the Holy Father in his struggle against Church dissenters. Nevertheless, Bishop Jones is also an administrator.

On one occasion, Bishop Jones and I were talking about his diocese. To my surprise, he said quite openly that he disagreed with certain policies of his own department heads. If that is so, I asked Bishop Jones, then why don't you change these policies? Bishop Jones responded that he never overruled a department head except in the area of finances. Thus, if the Rector of the Diocesan Seminary wanted a new program that involved the allocation of additional money the bishop would not hesitate to say no. Outside of finances, however, the bishop would not interfere with the policy of a department head even if he himself disapproved of that policy.

At first glance, it might seem that Bishop Jones was saying that money was the only important consideration. His actual attitude, however, was more complex. Further discussion revealed that he overruled on finances because he felt he could do so without creating an administrative uproar. The department heads might not like his decision but they still accepted his power in this area. They all recognized that there would be financial chaos unless somebody had the authority to bring diocesan expenditures into line with diocesan revenues.

In other words, the bishop acted on finances because that was the one area in which failing to act would cause far more administrative difficulties than acting. (By "administrative difficulties," I mean short-term, practical day-by-day problems.) In all other areas, the reverse was true. On these matters, acting would cause far more administrative problems than failing to act.

As Bishop Jones himself put it: "If I interfered with the policy decisions of my department heads, they would probably resign. Then who would I get? After all, a bishop has to fill these positions."

Strange as it seems, this is an attitude generally possessed by administrators. There are many slots that they are expected to fill. Keeping all the slots filled becomes an important preoccupation for the managers of organizations. What would it look like to yourself and to others if the management chart posted on the wall had holes in it?

To compound the administrative problem of slot-filling, some positions require special training. As an illustration, Bishop Jones pointed to his Catholic schools. The teachers in Catholic schools must be accredited by the state. If the teachers strike, the schools literally cannot function unless other accredited people can be found. While a bishop can ignore challenges or attacks from Catholics who do not occupy essential posts in the diocesan administrative structure, he cannot treat his teachers in the same way. Instead, he must negotiate with his teachers in order to satisfy their demands. To a great extent, they are independent of his control since they have built a power-base that enables them to close his Church institutions.

This example indicates the reason that some bishops are reluctant to challenge the dissenters but, in contrast, do not hesitate to stand up to loyal Catholics who are urging them to act. The traditional Catholics who are pleading with the bishop to stop dissent are not themselves in a position where they can close all Church institutions unless their request is satisfied. Administratively, therefore, they can be ignored. On the other hand, the dissenters *are* in such a crucial position, or so it seems to the bishop. Dissenting theologians can close his diocesan seminary and will, if he attempts to interfere with their assault on Church doctrine. Dissenting religious education teachers can close his schools. Dissenting priests and religious can close his parishes. Therefore, the bishop-administrator believes he must reach some agreement with the dissenters because they are so entrenched that they can prevent his organization from functioning unless he appeases them. And what is the agreement? To leave them alone; to permit them to continue their attacks on Church teaching; to look the other way.

Returning to Bishop Jones, he showed his concern for orthodoxy whenever a vacancy occurred and he had the chance to select a new department head. On one such occasion, he asked the newly appointed diocesan religious education director to come to his office for a private talk. Almost tearfully, Bishop Jones made an appeal for orthodoxy. "Please stress Catholic teaching more than has been done in the past," said Bishop Jones to his department head.

In summary, Bishop Jones apparently considered his position to be similar to that of the President when he chooses a Supreme Court Justice. Prior to making an appointment to the Court, a President tries to find a judge who will reflect his views. Once the selection has been made, however, the judges are free to do whatever they wish and the President has no power to interfere until the next Court vacancy occurs.

The Secondary Administrator

Before leaving the subject of Bishop Jones, let us consider how his religious education appointment turned out. What occurred (or better, what failed to occur) gives us another clue as to the reason that dissent continues to flourish in many dioceses.

Now it so happened that Bishop Jones had in fact succeeded in choosing a department head who shared his feelings about orthodoxy. Nevertheless, the hopes of Bishop Jones went unfulfilled. Instead of changing for the better, things in the religious education department went on much the same as before. Why? To understand the reason, let us consider the position in which "secondary administrators" find themselves.

We have said previously that in many dioceses the "secondary administrators" are practically autonomous (at least with respect to the bishop) when it comes to questions of policy. For instance, in most dioceses the bishop has little or no influence over what goes into the diocesan newspaper, even though the bishop is listed nominally as the publisher. The person who actually controls what goes into the newspaper is the editor, the "secondary administrator." In the same way, the people who control what takes place in diocesan religious education are the people whom the bishop has chosen to head this branch of his organization.

However, that last statement must be modified in one important respect. What has been said about the bishop is also true of the administrators of large diocesan departments. Like the bishop himself, these secondary administrators are afraid that if a conflict takes place their day-to-day organization may be disrupted. In addition, the secondary administrators have a further worry. If a conflict breaks out in their department, will not the bishop blame them for it?

The secondary administrators tend to think that one of the things the bishop most wants from them is to keep things quiet. As a result, even if the secondary administrators are themselves loyal to Church teaching, they are usually afraid to move against the dissenters within their department. The editor of the diocesan Catholic newspaper may himself be a strong supporter of Church doctrine, but he is reluctant to remove a columnist on that paper who ridicules Church doctrine almost every week. Why? Because, if the editor acted in this way, a huge uproar would occur, a controversy that could threaten his own editorship, an explosion that he believes the bishop would not want.

Bishop Jones told his newly appointed department head: "Please stress Catholic teaching more than has been done in the past," and he meant it. But the message actually received by his religious education coordinator was the following: Bishop Jones is afraid to move against the dissenters himself. He thinks they are too powerful. If they're too strong for him, can you imagine what they would do to me? My best bet is to act in exactly the manner that Bishop Jones himself does, i.e., make a personal statement in support of orthodoxy but allow the dissenters in my department the freedom to do as they wish. That way there will be no administrative uproar.

Is the administrative attitude of Bishop Jones unusual? No, it represents probably the most common position taken by bishops in today's Church. As further illustration, here is a brief report about another manager of a large diocese, Cardinal Smith.

Cardinal Smith, like Bishop Jones, is known for his strong personal support of traditional Catholic teaching. Again like Bishop Jones, he tries hard to appoint secondary administrators who share these views. But how does the Cardinal treat dissent? Recently a major secular newspaper interviewed priests in the Cardinal's own diocese on this very question. Here are some direct quotes from the article:

"The Cardinal prefers to work quietly behind the scenes, shaping policies over a long time and allowing considerable discussion among various church groups. His associates say he wants to believe the best about people. 'He wants to find good people to work with,' an official said, 'rather than take on the bad guys. He doesn't like to admit the existence of problems. He's the most ebullient man you'd meet.'

"Some church leaders say that the Cardinal dislikes confrontations and that his desire to find amicable solutions through lengthy consultations sometimes masks a quality of indecisiveness . . . he has been widely lauded for his efforts to unify a church still in the throes of the major changes introduced by the Second Vatican Council. . . .

"Some church officials point out that the day of the 'powerhouse,' as the chancery once was called, is over. 'If there was really a time when a fiat was acceptable,' said Bishop X, the Vicar General of the Archdiocese, 'that time is gone.'

"The Cardinal has impressed many Catholics with his sensitivity. The desire by some for a stronger voice is offset by the apparently deep reservoir of appreciation for those qualities that the Cardinal most easily exhibits. 'A lot of priests comment about his being a good religious leader,' said the Reverend Y, chairman of the Archdiocesan Senate of Clergy. 'He gives the image of a holy man and gives a lot of time to people's opinions. People can disagree with him and his attitude is to give equal play to that and not to put them down.'"

The cardinal's qualities, as described by the newspaper, are excellent in many ways, but it must be understood clearly that these very qualities make it unlikely that the Cardinal will ever take effective disciplinary action against Church dissenters.

Instead, according to the article, the Cardinal will tend to deny that the problem exists and, while strongly supporting Catholic teaching himself, will leave the dissenters free to campaign against Church doctrine.

If the newspaper article is correct, other Church officials are constantly praising the Cardinal for employing restraint in dealing with the dissenters. Such restraint is considered to be a virtue and is even identified with the holiness. And, purely on an administrative level, the policy is certainly a wise one. The dissenters would revolt if the Cardinal attempted to take strong action. But why should they revolt if they are allowed to do whatever they want?

Such a policy produces the immediate benefit of administrative peace in the management of the diocese. The only problem is that (as described in our previous chapter), what is best administratively in the short-run is not always what is best doctrinally in the long-run. And that leads us to an important question.

Why?

Why can't the short-range policy that avoids disruption also be the best long-range policy? Why does the toleration of dissent almost always make things worse in the long-run instead of better, as desired by the well-meaning fathers, administrators, and bishops who adopt this policy? To understand the reason, let us quote two very different sources. The first is a poem written centuries ago. The second is a recent scientific study. Despite their differences, they both give us the same message.

In the 18th century, Alexander Pope wrote the following:

"Vice is a monster of so frightful mien
As to be hated needs but to be seen
Yet seen too oft, familiar with her face,
We first endure, then pity, then embrace."
—"Essay on Man," Epistle 2, Line 217

Whenever an evil first appears on the scene, it is usually recognized immediately for what it actually is. Instinctively, good people recoil from it. Their reaction is one of shock and disgust. However, if the evil is allowed to linger, if the evil stays around long enough to establish itself as a custom, then more and more people (including very good people) will fail to recognize it as wrong. What once produced disgust now produces no adverse reaction at all.

To quote another poet, this time a song-writer from the 20th century:

"In olden days a glimpse of stocking
Was looked on as something shocking
But now—heaven knows!
Anything goes."
—(Cole Porter)

As Alexander Pope indicates, the toleration of evil often passes through several stages. In the first stage, the evil is still recognized for what it is, but a decision is made to tolerate it for what seems to be a good practical reason. ("We first endure.")

In what can be a remarkably short time, however, the attitude of "endurance" gives way to sympathy ("then pity") and finally to acceptance ("then embrace"). A father may well have started by regarding his son Jim's "live-in" relationship with his girl friend as highly objectionable. Fearing the results of a direct confrontation, however, he decides to "endure" the situation because of what he considers to be a good practical reason, namely, that Jim will leave the house if the father does otherwise. Come back in a year's time and you will frequently hear such a father remark: "You know, at first I objected very much but now I feel it's really not so wrong after all, as long as they love each other. Besides, she's a nice girl."

What was regarded as blatantly immoral behavior is now viewed as more or less acceptable, certainly nothing to get excited about.

And that's the way it is with dissent within the Church. Endure it for the "best of practical reasons," and you will find in ten years' time, that it is a hundred times more entrenched than it was before.

A Scientific Study

What was grasped intuitively by 18th century poets is now being confirmed by a number of modern sociologists. As an illustration, here is an excerpt that I read recently in a prominent magazine. The magazine was reporting on an exhaustive study of American society recently published by one of the country's most prestigious sociologists. And what did the sociologist find?

> To sustain a social law or rule, violations must be kept rare, usually below the 2% level. When the rate of violations rises to 30% or higher—violent crime in poor neighborhoods, tax cheating, fraud and abuses at nursing homes—those who still bother to obey the laws begin to feel foolish.
>
> One common political practice of many administrators must be stopped: keeping laws on the books but ignoring their enforcement because of the difficulties involved. Even minor rules and mores, when routinely unenforced, promote disrespect and social disintegration. Thus, newspapers have reported what everyone already knows: a surprising

number of drivers now routinely go through red lights and stop signs. Rules in general—whether minor or major— from speeding and double parking to paying taxes—should either be dropped or more widely enforced. Carelessness about the proper enforcement of rules and regulations can shred the social contract.

The application to the Catholic Church is clear. Prior to the Second Vatican Council, dissent was well below the "2% level." It is no longer so low. Faced with widespread dissent, there has been an equally widespread decision by Church administrators that the best policy in the practical order is to issue a statement supporting the Church's position but to avoid the enforcement of that position since any attempt to do so would lead to a disruptive conflict with the dissenters. If the sociological study is correct, the results of such a policy will be increasing "social disintegration." And how very, very true it is to say that those Catholics "who still bother to obey the laws begin to feel foolish."

Four Categories of Bishops

The four different explanations can be summarized as follows:

Category I: Knowledge—Acceptance—No action: The bishops know about the problem of dissent but do not act because, either openly or tacitly, they approve of dissent, or at least consider dissent to be an acceptable option for Catholics.

Category II: No knowledge—No acceptance—No action: The bishops do not act because they are not aware (or at least they are not fully aware) of all the things the dissenters are doing.

Category III: Knowledge—No acceptance—But no action: The bishops know about the problem, do not approve dissent, but do not act because they believe:
   a) they are largely powerless;
   b) they would look foolish if they attempted to check dissent;
   c) attempts to check dissent would only boomerang and create more sympathy for those opposing the Pope;
   d) attempts to check dissent would be a *pastoral* mistake (i.e., it would lead to a tremendous institutional upheaval against the bishop with an open revolt very likely . . . a deliberate decision by the bishop to ignore the pro-

blem prevents an open revolt and brings about a surface peace);

f) avoidance of the problem must be the best policy since it is what the other bishops are doing.

Category IV: Knowledge—No Acceptance—Some action: The bishops know about the problem and do not approve of dissent, but believe they are taking effective action:

a) by their own personal statements in support of Church teachings;

b) by efforts that take place "behind the scenes."

We have already spent much time describing Category III, those bishops who know about dissent and who are personally strong supporters of Church doctrine but who do not act to check dissent. Here let us say a few words about the other three categories.

Category I: Knowledge—Acceptance—No action.

The bishops know, but do not act to check dissent, because they approve.

The first thing that can be said about this category is that it is radically different from the other three. In Categories II, III, and IV, the bishops do not approve of dissent. A Category I bishop does approve.

That is the reason that the statement was made a moment ago that a particular bishop might be influenced by three of the categories, but not by all four. A bishop loyal to the Pope, for example, might know some of the activities of the dissenters but be in the dark about other things. With respect to what he knows, he may take certain steps that he believes will be effective but avoid other actions that might create what he considers to be serious administrative problems. Such a bishop is influenced to some extent by Category II (as to what he does not know), by Category III (as to the actions he avoids) and by Category IV (as to the steps he does take).

But Category I stands alone and we must ask two questions about it: First, can such bishops exist? Second, do they in fact exist at present?

The answer to the first question is clear enough. While we believe Christ will always be with the Church, it has in fact happened that the whole nations have broken away from the Catholic Church and that they have been led in this revolt by their own bishops. England at the time of Henry VIII provides a striking example. Only one Bishop remained faithful. All the other prelates became "Category I" bishops.

The answer to the second question is not so clear. What the future may hold is unknown, but at the moment of this writing it would be hard to find a single American bishop who publicly disputes the Pope on a question of faith or morals. Almost universally, the bishops proclaim their personal support for the official Church teaching. Therefore, if Category I bishops do exist, one of the things they are now doing is to deceive the Vatican about their actual positions.

Since one naturally wishes to believe the best about bishops and not the worst, the assumption of this book is that their statements of personal support for Church teaching should be taken at face value and presumed to be true. At the same time, however, the author must acknowledge that dioceses do exist in which despite the bishop's profession of personal orthodoxy, dissent is not only tolerated but to all outward appearances encouraged. In such dioceses, dissenters are elevated consistently to key positions while priests considered too orthodox (whatever that phrase means) and frequently labelled as "fundamentalist" or "Jansenist," are admonished and even harrassed by their bishop (the very same bishop who assured the Pope of his own orthodoxy).

If Category I bishops do exist, one truth must always be kept in mind. No bishop has the authority to order any Catholic to act against Catholic doctrine on faith or morals. With respect to purely Church laws (Note: see my *Defending the Papacy* for a discussion of the difference between doctrine and discipline, between what can be changed and what cannot), a bishop is sometimes given the authority to modify them if conditions in his area seem to warrant it. If the bishop is not given this option, then he is obliged to follow the Vatican direction. If the bishop takes a contrary action, *no Catholic has any obligation to follow him on this matter.*

Category II: No knowledge—No acceptance—No actions.

The bishops do not know what is happening.

This explanation may be divided into two sections. First, it may mean that the bishops literally do not know. This is frequently assumed to be the case by loyal Catholics when they first encounter dissent. They say to themselves: "If only the bishop knew, he would so something." if they tell him and there is still no action that they can see, the loyal Catholics can early become disillusioned and adopt Explanation 1—that the bishop must approve of what is happening.

The "does not know" view is sometimes supported by action of the dissenters themselves. Occasionally a diocesan official who dissents from Church teaching will tell his audience: "Turn off the tape recorders at this point." Once that is done, the priest or religious will express opposition to the official Church teaching. Why request that the tape recorders be turned off unless there is a fear that the bishop might act if he knew what was really happening? One dissenter put things bluntly. "If the bishop even knew one-quarter of what goes on within our diocese, he would have a heart attack!"

In addition to the explanation that the bishop literally does not know, there is a second aspect to the "does not know" category. The bishop may know theoretically what is happening but he may not realize the devastating effect dissent is having on the people within his diocese. He knows in a vague and abstract way about the existence of dissent, but he is not really sensitive to the needs of his people—not appreciative of what dissent is doing to them.

Sometimes it may be that loyal Catholics do not bring the problem to his attention. Or, if they do, it is only a handful of loyal Catholics who express themselves. Ninety-nine percent of those who are affected never think of telling the bishop what is happening to them.

A second reason the bishop may not realize what is happening is that those in charge of his programs will often deny that they are affected by dissent. They assure the bishop that things are going well. With such assurances, the bishop will dismiss any letters of protest as only an isolated instance or as a report that cannot possibly be true.

A third reason the bishop may not be sensitive to the effect of dissent on loyal Catholics is that he himself is not so affected. When a person does not experience something himself, it is easy to overlook what others are experiencing, especially if these other people are not active in telling him what is happening to them.

For example, a person in the best of health can find it very difficult to be aware of the feelings of sick people. Intellectually, he knows that they are sick. Intellectually, he knows that sick people often have feelings of great frustration. However, it is only when he himself becomes sick, when he himself experiences the same feelings of frustration, that he really appreciates their attitude. (At least that is the case with many of us. There are those who although not sick themselves have worked hard to become fully sensitive to the feelings of the sick. Most of us, however, try to help sick people but tend not to appreciate their frustrations until we ourselves experience the same thing.)

It should always be remembered that the bishops themselves are the one group of people who do not have to listen to the dissenters. They can, if they so wish, isolate themselves from dissent. For that very reason, they do not experience what many loyal Catholics experience on the parish level, the way that dissent is used to ridicule the faith and rip people away from their beliefs.

In summary, Category II assumes either that the bishops do not know the dimensions of what is going on or that, while having a theoretical knowledge, they do not realize the effect of dissent on loyal Catholics because they are not sensitive to their feelings and experiences.

Category IV: Knowledge—No acceptance—Some action.

The bishops know and believe that they are acting effectively, that they do not approve of dissent.

In this category, the bishops are attempting to act in support of Church doctrine. These bishops believe they are having an impact because of the statements that they personally make on behalf of Church teaching. They may also be active behind the scenes, calling in the dissenters and emphasizing to them the importance of supporting the official Church teaching.

What evidence is there to support the belief that some bishops may be trying to act against dissent "behind-the-scenes?" Basically, what we have are statements by the dissenters themselves.

If one listens closely to Church dissenters, they seem to be saying that (from their point of view) there are "good" bishops and "bad" bishops. On the one hand, a favorite trick of some Church dissenters is to employ a kind of psychological warfare against loyal Catholics by relating so-called "private conversations" that the dissenters have had with certain bishops who are usually unidentified. According to the dissenters, the unidentified bishops tell them secretly: "We're really with you, but we can't say so publicly." If such accounts are true, and not simply a lie told either to discourage orthodox Catholics or to give the dissenters added prestige by creating the impression that they are "buddy-buddy" with certain members of the American hierarchy, then it would mean that a number of bishops belong to Category I and are deceiving the Holy Father about their views.

While praising these "good" bishops, however, the dissenters also lash out at other bishops who are accused of doing "terrible" things to check dissent. For example, one priest dissenter revealed in his newspaper column that some "unenlightened" bishops were even having personal conversations with their seminarians prior to ordination in order to make certain that these seminarians supported the Pope and Catholic doctrine. A second priest-dissenter, only weeks after telling his readers that "good bishops" supported him, launched a strong attack against "sneaky bishops" who were trying to enforce "the dictates of Rome." A third dissenter, a prominent Scripture scholar, compared these "bad" bishops to "a drunken father" whom "we try to hide when company comes, and we worry about what half-wit blunders he will make next."

Would such vicious comments be made if the bishops were secretly in league with the dissenters or even if they were letting them alone? It appears unlikely. At least a few bishops must be attempting to do something behind-the-scenes but, precisely because their activity is hidden, loyal Catholics usually know nothing about it.

Somewhat more "out-in-the-open" are the personal statements issued by many bishops in support of orthodox Catholic doctrine. Unfortunately, such statements usually have little impact on the local parish level. Part of the problem may be the slowness of a bureaucracy in responding to the wishes of the person on the top, especially when those who are in "middle management" positions disagree with what the person at the top wants to accomplish. In addition, the bishops, despite some excellent statements, often give the implementation of these statements over to those who disagree with what they have said.

One example of this occurred some years ago when the bishops of the United States debated a proposed statement on religious education. After seeing the initial draft (which had been prepared for the bishops by religious education "experts"), a number of the bishops wanted the statement to be much stronger in emphasizing how important it was for all teachers to obey the authority of the Pope and to stress orthodox Catholic doctrine in their religious education programs. They even wanted to encourage students to memorize part of the catechism, as had been done in the past.

As a result, these bishops suggested certain changes in the document. Although their proposals were resisted vigorously by the religious educators who had produced the original version, the bishops who wanted doctrine emphasized succeeded in persuading a majority of their colleagues to make important changes in the religious education document.

The time and effort given to this matter shows clearly that many bishops were very concerned about Catholic doctrine. Yet, when the debate was all over, the document was then given to the religious educators to implement in their dioceses—the very religious educators who had strenuously resisted the changes. The outcome? Despite the fine statement, those parts of the document that were at variance with the attitude of the people who were actually implementing the program (namely, the religious educators) were never carried out and simply became dead letters. Thus, we see the gap between what is said by the bishops in their statements and what is actually put into practice by those who are given the responsibility of implementing the program.

We have just illustrated something that often happens to those who head large organizations. What we are really considering is this question: How can people think they are acting and assume they are having a significant effect—when they are really having little or no impact?

Perhaps it can best be explained by an example. Imagine that you drop a rock into a pond. Let us make it a fairly large rock so that it takes a certain amount of effort for you to carry it to the pond and to throw it into the water. You drop this one-hundred pound rock into the pond and there is a tremendous splash all around you. But, even though there is a great splash next to you, the dropping of that large rock into the water has no effect at all on ninety-nine percent of the pond. Why? Because of the size of the pond. No matter how big the rock, and no matter how much effort you yourself put into it, the pond is so large that the effect is felt only very close to you, that is, only very close to the source of the effort. In contrast, if you were dealing with a very small organization, if you dropped such a rock into a bathtub, then it would certainly be true that you would have a huge effect upon the entire body of water. However, this is not true with a large organization because of the size involved.

In a large organization, for an action to have any effect beyond its own immediate circle, it must be picked up and reinforced in much the way that a booster reinforces the original source of power. And that was the purpose of Church institutions, to pick up what was being said by the Pope and the bishops and to reinforce them on the local level. But if Church institutions do not do this, then even the statements of the Pope himself will not be passed on as they should be to Catholics living in parishes and attending Catholic schools. Without this reinforcement, any action by a Church official, even a Pope or bishop, will tend to have an effect limited to those with whom the Pope or the bishop is immediately in contact.

As we have seen earlier, the problem with Church institutions at present (especially educational institutions) is that a great number of people in "middle management" positions not only do not support but disagree with Church teaching. So long as this problem remains, the personal actions by the man at the top are likely to have only a small effect upon the

Catholics in his diocese. His initiatives run into a stone wall at the middle management level and cannot get through that wall to reach Catholics at the grass roots.

However, it is often true that this barrier is not seen clearly by the person who is at the top. Like a speaker who does not realize he is talking into a dead microphone because he himself can hear his voice very well, the one at the top thinks he is being effective. After all, to return to our example of the pond, the person at the top lives in the one area where his dropping of the stone has a big impact. Furthermore, the person at the top knows all the effort that went into carrying that stone to the pond. He sees the water around him move considerably. Because of what he personally observes, he finds it hard to believe those reports that come in from people who are 100 or 200 yards away, people who keep insisting that nothing has actually happened. He may even feel a little insulted at the statements of these people. He simply cannot put himself into their positions because he does not live in their environment. Conversely, the people who are some distance away from him do not even realize that he has made a tremendous personal effort in dropping the stone because they do not see even a ripple in the places where they themselves reside.

A final element is that the close advisors of the person at the top almost always assure him that he is in fact doing very well and exerting a considerable influence. Perhaps these advisors themselves believe this since they live in the same neighborhood as the person at the top. Even if they do not, even if they themselves realize that the actions of the man at the top are having relatively little impact outside the immediate circle, they will often hesitate to tell this to their chief. They hesitate out of a mistaken sense of loyalty. They feel that any statement will come across as criticism of their boss. It may depress the man at the top or even make him angry. Perhaps the advisors will lose their own positions if they speak the truth bluntly, since they will be looked on as the bearers of bad news. Therefore, they heap congratulations on their chief for his effort. This reinforcement, these congratulations by those around him, persuades the person at the top more than ever that he is accomplishing what should be done. Confirmed in such an attitude, he will simply not believe those who report otherwise. "They do not know what they are talking about."

9.
Why Do The Bishops Not Promote Church Teaching Themselves?

What we have been concentrating on to this point is the attitude of the bishops towards dissent. We have given four different explanations why this dissent is often unchecked on the local level. However, a very different question could well be asked. Even if the bishops are unable to check dissent, why are they not far more active in promoting the true Catholic teaching?

This question was raised recently by a Catholic editor who is very loyal to the bishops. Nevertheless, the editor pointed out that, since the issuance of Pope Paul's encyclical on birth control, virtually nothing had been done by the American bishops to promote the Pope's teaching. While the dissenters were undertaking extensive efforts to undermine the Pope on this matter, the bishops simply made one statement of support and then did nothing else.

It is not simply the issue of contraception that has been treated in this manner. Many other Church teachings have been handled in a similar way. The relative inactivity of the bishops with respect to doctrinal matters is all the more striking when compared to the actions of the Pope on doctrine and to the actions of the bishops themselves on administrative questions. If one were to study the statements of recent Popes, one would see a strong and continuous emphasis on Church doctrine, especially doctrines that are being challenged by Church dissenters. Again and again the Popes speak out in support of these teachings. In contrast, if one were to conduct a similar study with respect to the statements of most American bishops, one would find that this doctrinal emphasis was absent. It is not that the personal statements of the bishops deny Church doctrine. It is simply that these subjects are rarely, if ever, mentioned.

The individual statements of the American bishops may contain many good things. For instance, they usually appeal to Catholics to love God and to love their fellow men. Unlike the Pope, however, the statements of a typical American bishop will not discuss the doctrine of the inerrancy of Sacred Scripture, or the doctrine of the Real Presence of Jesus in the Eucharist, or the doctrine of Papal infallibility, or any of the other doctrines that are being challenged by Church dissenters. If one were to ask the bishops whether they believed in these teachings, they would respond: "Of course we do." But they do not talk about them very much. Thus, while the Pope uses his sermons and addresses both to teach doctrine and to encourage Catholics to be good, the American bishops use their sermons and addresses only to encourage Catholics to be good.

The inactivity of the bishops on doctrine contrasts not only with the efforts of the Pope, but with the efforts of the bishops themselves on matters of administration. When a bishop is challenged on an administrative decision that he himself has made, i.e., when "dissenters" to that decision begin to make their presence felt in his diocese, the bishop often responds by becoming very energetic in support of his decision. Instead of being content with a single statement, the bishop is determined to "outwork" the dissenters. If they are going to be active in dissenting from his administrative authority, he will be even more active in promoting that authority. In such a situation, it is not unusual for a bishop to go from group to group within his diocese in order to make a personal appeal for support. He is determined to "sell" his decision to the Catholic people and to obtain their backing.

As one example, a controversy recently arose in a diocese involving an administrative decision by the bishop to spend a million dollars in renovating the cathedral. A number of lay people protested this decision. They argued that the money involved should have been given to the poor. The bishop responded by appearing personally before more than twenty key groups in his diocese in order to explain the reason for his action and appeal for their backing. His efforts were unceasing as he used every opportunity to build up support for this administrative decision.

In the same diocese there is also a strong dissent against some of the doctrinal and moral teachings of the Holy Father. In contrast to his energetic efforts on the administrative matter, the local bishop has done nothing to defend the Pope's teaching except to issue one statement saying that he himself agrees with Church doctrine.

I believe it is this striking contrast that many loyal Catholics notice instinctively in their parishes and schools. The irony is that, despite all the talk about the "freedom to dissent," there usually is little freedom to dissent from local *administrative* decisions even if such decisions have been made by Church dissenters themselves in situations where they are in charge of a local or diocesan program. Thus, many diocesan newspapers will routinely carry columns or letters challenging doctrines emphasized by the Pope and, despite appeals by the Apostolic Delegate, will continue to do so. But these same papers frequently will refuse to publish columns or letters that challenge administrative decisions made by local authorities.

One cannot dissent from local administrative decisions, but one can dissent from the doctrinal decisions of the highest Authority in the Church! Seeing this, is it any wonder that some Catholics assume that the doctrinal teachings must be unimportant? After all, the general rule followed in many organizations is that people must accept what is essential to that organization but are allowed the "freedom to dissent" in non-essential areas. In today's Church, this general rule is turned topsy-turvy. Instead of unity on essentials and freedom on non-essentials, those who challenge the Pope offer Catholics "freedom" on essentials (doctrine) but demand conformity on non-essentials (their own administrative decisions).

While Catholics should follow the administrative decisions of local Church authorities (provided, of course, that these decisions are in conformity with Church doctrine and the directives of higher Church authorities), they should also be given a wide-ranging freedom to ask questions about such administrative decisions, even those made by the local bishop himself. Why? Because the rightness or wrongness of these "practical" or "administrative" decisions is not guaranteed in any way by God. As we saw in *Defending the Papacy*, the only guidance God certainly provides the Church on such matters is that no administrative decision by the Holy Father will ever result in the elimination of anything essential to the Church. While this limited guarantee exists with respect to the administrative decisions of the Pope, no guarantee of any kind exists with regard to the administrative decisions of local ecclesiastical authorities.

As a result, the practical or administrative decisions of local authorities can turn out to be more harmful than helpful. They can be changed, and should be subject to constant review. As part of the consultation process involved in this review, Catholics should normally be given considerable latitude to question administrative decisions, although this should always be done in a respectful way.

When it comes to doctrine, however, the principle involved is very different. As the Church officially teaches, the Pope has the authority to make final and binding decisions on doctrine. When he does, all Catholics have an obligation to obey, and our obligation comes from the fundamental teaching that the Holy Spirit will guide the Pope in such a situation.

Why Does the Current Situation Exist?

If it is true that the American bishops will promote their own administrative decisions energetically and personally, then why do they not act in a similar way on questions of doctrine? It cannot be fear of an explosion in their diocese. Such fear could well explain why the bishops do not attempt to stop dissent. But here we are talking about promoting the good, not about stopping the bad.

One possible explanation is that the bishops do not care about doctrine. While this may be true with respect to Category I bishops, I know personally that there are many bishops who do care, but who still do not act as the Pope does on doctrine or as they themselves do on administrative matters.

I believe that the inactivity of the bishops on doctrine can be explained to great extent by something that sociologists refer to as "cultural lag." The term "culture" refers to a society. When sociologists speak about a "lag" in a society, what they mean is that a certain pattern once existed. This pattern has now changed. It no longer exists as it did previously. Nevertheless, many people within the society continue to assume that the previous pattern is still in effect. Therefore, they act in a way that would be effective if this previous pattern did in fact exist, but is not now effective because the previous pattern is gone. In other words, there is a "lag" in the sense that their present actions presume a pattern that has now gone out of existence.

Two Examples

Before considering cultural lag as it applies to the action of the bishops on Church doctrine, let us give two other illustrations of cultural lag in order to present a clearer picture of what it means. After the Civil War, there was a great development of the factory system in the United States. The introduction of complex machinery brought about a situation in which industrial accidents sharply increased. However, it was not until 1911 that the States began to respond to this new problem by passing workmen's compensation laws. The period between 1865 and 1911 was a period of cultural lag. The problem existed. To an outside observer it might have appeared that nobody cared since no action was being taken to respond to the problem. However, the actual truth was a little different. The reason for the inactivity was that a new pattern had suddenly emerged and it took American society a period of time to figure out how to operate effectively under the new pattern. During the 50 years of "cultural lag," the states continued to act as if the previous pattern were still in existence, the pattern in which there was no need for workmen's compensation laws. Until people realized that a very different situation now confronted them, they were not able to make any progress in solving the problem.

In *Defending the Papacy* we gave yet another example of cultural lag, although we did not use the term at that time. We wrote about the role of judges in our country. The Supreme Court was created to tell people what the law was, not to tell people what the law should be. For that reason, judges were removed from the normal checks of the political process since their personal views were considered to be irrelevant. Their "likes" or "dislikes" did not matter because the judges were supposed to be fact-finders who would study what the law actually was and then inform society about what they had found.

That was the original pattern. In practice, however, as many legal scholars themselves admit, a very different pattern began to emerge. Supreme Court judges began to be legislators. They were not content simply to say what the law was. Instead, they wanted to tell society what the law should be. Thus, those judges who declared unconstitutional laws protecting the unborn child were taking their own personal preferences and using the power they possessed to impose their views on the rest of society. In *Defending the Papacy*, we quoted Justice Frankfurter and Justice Hughes, both of whom stated that this is in fact how the Court operates.

Yet those who want to protest what the Supreme Court has done often find themselves powerless. Why? Because the Court is still protected from public opinion since the laws of our country and the attitude of many people still presume that the judges are not doing what in fact they are. That is what Justice Frankfurter meant when he remarked that people have been taught to believe that, when the Court speaks, it *is* the Constitution, whereas, in reality, it is not the Constitution but their own personal ideas. Frankfurter thought that if the runaway power of the Courts were ever to be checked, the public must realize that the previous pattern had changed and now a very new pattern existed. Otherwise, they would continue to be powerless to solve the problem. They would be helpless precisely because they would be victims of a "cultural lag" in believing that a pattern still existed when in fact it once had been present but was now gone.

With these two examples of cultural lag—how cultural lag kept the States from meeting the problem of injuries to workmen and how cultural lag still keeps people in our society from meeting the problem of legislation imposed by our judges—let us consider how cultural lag applies to the bishops. In what way does cultural lag keep the bishops from acting effectively in the promotion of Church doctrine?

To begin with, what was the previous pattern within the American Church? The previous pattern, the one in which almost all American bishops were trained, was for the bishop himself to concentrate on the administrative and practical aspects of the diocese while delegating the promotion of Church teaching to specialists who were known as theologians. This pattern of delegating to others the responsibility to defend Church teaching worked very well, so long as the theologians were themselves loyal to the Church's teaching.

However, that situation has now changed radically. Instead of being loyal to the Church's teaching, many of the specialists are now far more loyal to the dissenters or to their own ideas. Nevertheless, despite the fact that a new pattern has emerged, the personal actions of most bishops still presume that the old pattern continues to exist and that the defense of Church teachings will be taken care of by specialists while the bishops will concentrate on the administrative and the practical. It is because the activity of the bishops has not yet changed so as to reflect the new situation, because they are still doing what was effective when their specialists were loyal, that bishops pass fine statements in support of Church teaching but then leave the implementation of these statements to specialists who disagree with what they have said. They do this because that is the way the bishops have always operated in the past, to make a statement of principle and then leave it to the specialists to put it into effect.

It is for a similar reason that a bishop can make a personal statement in support of Church doctrine and fail to realize the importance of working constantly to "sell" the Church's teaching to Catholics on the local level. The bishop does not recognize a need for such promotion because in the past it was all done automatically by Church institutions. In the past it was not necessary for a bishop to undertake a personal and energetic effort in support of Catholic doctrine.

However, things are very different in the present. Hopefully, bishops who believe strongly in traditional Church teaching will come to realize that if (for whatever reasons) they believe they cannot stop dissent, then they have to compensate for the existence of dissent by their own unceasing promotion of Catholic doctrine. A simple statement every ten or fifteen years will have no impact whatever.

Finally, it should be noted that bishops loyal to Church doctrine are by no means the only Catholics victimized by "cultural lag." Lay people faithful to the Church can be (and often are) affected by the same phenomenon. We have previously written about the tragedy that afflicts many families. Men and women who believe in Catholic teaching with all their hearts send their sons and daughters to "Catholic" schools or "Catholic" religious education programs, often making a considerable financial sacrifice to do so. They make these sacrifices because they assume automatically that these schools will do for their children what they once did for them—namely, confirm them in the Faith by promoting Church doctrine. Instead, as Archbishop Sheen stated, the schools promote dissent from Church doctrine. Influenced by the atmosphere at these schools, the sons and daughters begin to abandon Catholic practices and the parents are heart-broken. Like many bishops, the loyal parents often feel personally powerless in such a situation.

This is "cultural lag," acting on the assumption that a pattern which once existed is still in effect even though in fact it is not. Nobody (whether bishop, priest, religious, or lay person) should be embarrassed to have been victimized by cultural lag. At one time or another, it happens to all of us. Nevertheless, it is important to know about cultural lag, since faithful Catholics will then realize the necessity to adopt a new pattern of behavior in order to respond effectively to the changing conditions that have produced a "new pattern of dissent." By a "new pattern of behavior" for loyal Catholics, I mean that bishops can no longer assume automatically that their specialists will promote Catholic doctrine, and parents can no longer assume automatically that "Catholic" schools will promote Catholic doctrine. Instead, bishops and parents and all faithful Catholics must assume that exactly the opposite will frequently occur, and this means that bishops and parents and all faithful Catholics must themselves take on the personal responsibility of promoting Catholic teaching, a responsibility they did not have to assume under the old pattern.

How faithful Catholics can do all this will be the subject of the next book. For now, we are simply discussing why a new behavior pattern must be adopted. The situation is not unlike that which occurs when a hitherto unknown disease suddenly appears upon the scene. Because of "medical lag," there is a period of time during which the disease exists but no cure has been found. During that period, the illness rages unchecked. Nevertheless, with enough hard work by the medical community, an effective remedy is eventually found. As the saying goes, we must pray as if everything depended upon God but work as if everything depended upon ourselves. If enough faithful Catholics act in this way, then an effective cure will be found and the present terrible disease of dissent will no longer rage unchecked.

Conclusion

As we conclude this section on the bishops, it might be stated that the explanations given here apply also to others who exercise authority within the Church. Their general attitude is to make statements in support of the Church's teaching, their own personal statements. At the same time, for the reasons expressed previously, little or nothing, and certainly nothing effective, is done to check the power of the dissenters within the Church.

When Catholic laity urge the bishops to check dissent, those in authority will usually respond politely until the point is reached where they feel they are being pushed to do something they have decided not to do. Then (like the father in our example) the bishops frequently "push back" and express their annoyance at those who are pleading with them for action. The result is that two groups of people who support the Church's teaching (the bishops and Catholics who want Church doctrine taught in their parishes) end up in a tragic fight with each other while the dissenters continue on their merry way.

Here, if I may be so bold, I would like to say a word to the American bishops. Throughout this section I have tried to discuss the many reasons that some of you have given to me for the apparent inaction of local Church authorities in the face of the assault on Catholic doctrine. I have tried as hard as I can to do this without any spirit of antagonism or hostility or even disappointment toward those who are exercising authority in this way. I have discussed the reasons for your present course of action, in that it can appear to be both the pastoral way to treat dissenters and the correct administrative way to avoid disturbance in the short-run.

At the same time, I have tried to portray the way your seeming inaction appears to many loyal Catholics who desperately want to live in an atmosphere that strongly affirms Church doctrine, but who do not because of the dissenters. These Catholics cry out and they are often angry. While I do not excuse their anger, while I would strongly recommend that they adopt a different tone, it should be recognized that they are rightly upset and frustrated because they are like a person who needs air but who is suffocating. What they are trying to tell you is that they are drowning. Would you tell a drowning man: "Be a little more polite in your requests or I will not listen?" If their tone of anger causes you, their spiritual fathers, to turn a deaf ear to them, then (understand it well) you are allowing them to suffocate because they have annoyed you.

I realize that often you may not understand how these loyal Catholics feel. Perhaps it is our fault for either not expressing it to you at all or not expressing it properly. In that case, the following example may help to illustrate what kind of message many loyal Catholics are presently receiving from your policies (even though it may not be the message that you intend to send).

Imagine a father who tells his children to go to Mass but does not attend himself. What are his children likely to do in such a situation? They are receiving mixed signals. The words say one thing, but the action of their father says something very different. In such a circumstance, they are likely to follow his actions—in this case, his failure to attend Mass. That will be more important to the children than the words.

At present this is the way things often appear to loyal Catholics. But let us take the example of the father a bit further. Suppose that he has a good reason for not attending Mass. As an example, let us imagine that he has a severe case of claustrophobia, a fear of crowds that is so great that it is a legitimate excusing reason for not attending Mass on Sunday. If the children knew about his claustrophobia, then they would not be "scandalized." They would no longer think that his failure to go to Mass means that he does not care.

However, the father does not want to tell them. Why? One reason may be simply embarrassment. After all, a father is not supposed to have such a weakness. Furthermore, how very embarrassing it must be to tell one's own children about this problem, especially if his children look on their father with awe and reverence. Therefore, he does not tell them. Instead he hides the problem from them. As a result, even though the father's decision to conceal his difficulty is a very human reaction, the children end up with an impression that is far, far worse. They know their father is staying away from Mass and they naturally assume that he could go if he wished, so they conclude that he does not care.

I believe this example could appropriately be applied to the present relationship between the bishops and many faithful Catholics. Therefore, my word to the bishops is: Please do not hesitate to reveal to the Catholic community what your true problem is. If the reason that you do not act to stop dissent is the belief that you yourself are powerless, then tell this bluntly to the Catholic people. Otherwise, the average loyal Catholic will never realize that you consider yourself powerless, just as this average child will not realize that his father has claustrophobia unless the father reveals his actual condition. I appreciate that it is most embarrassing to make such a public admission to the Catholics of your diocese since a bishop is not supposed to be powerless. It comes across as a weakness. For that reason, the natural inclination is to hide it. But, if you do, your inaction will inevitably appear to be tacit approval of dissent and indifference toward Catholic doctrine. Which is more important: that you avoid embarrassment or that you keep your Catholic people from being scandalized?

Finally, would it be possible for you to re-examine the situation to see whether you really are powerless to act? Could you please look at the long-range consequences of allowing dissent to continue? If you still feel that you cannot move against dissent, is there not something extra that you can do to promote Church teaching? The faithful need such activity by you very badly, even while many of us are prepared to do whatever we can do on our own to work for Catholic teaching. You are our bishops. We are your people. Please help us to preserve our Faith.

10.
May Loyal Catholics Disagree with Church Authorities on Questions of Strategy?

This chapter is addressed to faithful Catholics. It attempts to answer a question that may have come to you as you read the last section on the bishops. The question is this: do we have a right to disagree with the decision of the bishops to tolerate dissent? If we disagree, are we not doing exactly what we question in the Church dissenters, that is, challenging the authority of the bishops?

This is an objection that dissenters themselves often throw at orthodox Catholics. For instance, one prominent Church dissenter recently suggested in his diocesan newspaper column that loyal Catholics who questioned the tolerance of dissent by their bishop were guilty of disobedience. In another column, the same dissenter justified his own disobedience on Church doctrine by referring to St. Paul the Apostle. He claimed that St. Paul stood up publicly to St. Peter, the first Pope. Therefore, he concluded, it must be permissible for him and his fellow dissenters to stand up publicly to the present Pope on Church doctrine. Let us attempt to answer these two arguments of the dissenters.

First, are we doing the same thing as the dissenters if we question the practical decision made by many bishops to tolerate dissent? The answer is a definite no. Here it might be helpful to refer to the first book in this series, *Defending the Papacy*, in which we discussed the authority of the Pope and the different kinds of statements the Pope or the bishops can make. (See also the paragraphs contrasting administrative decisions with doctrinal decisions that appear in the preceding chapter of this book.)

As we saw in both these places, infallibility, the guarantee of the Holy Spirit to the Pope and to the bishops when they are united to the Pope, pertains *only* to questions of faith and morals. It does *not* pertain to questions of Church discipline or to practical judgments the Church authorities may make as to what is the best course of action to pursue at a particular time in order to reach the desired goal. We must always distinguish between the doctrinal or moral teaching involved and the practical decision that is made about the best way to operate in order to promote this teaching.

As we saw in *Defending the Papacy*, even with respect to doctrinal or moral teaching there are occasions when it is presented in such a way that it is not intended to be binding. We use the phrase "obiter dicta" to refer to statements made "by the way." There is also such a thing as provisional teaching. Nevertheless, even when we are talking about certain and binding Church teaching (and that is what we are talking about when we refer to many of the doctrines that the dissenters deny), we must make the distinction between the teaching itself and the judgment about the best practical course of action to follow in order to promote the teaching.

It is only the teaching itself whose truth is guaranteed by God. With respect to practical judgments about the best policy to pursue in order to promote a teaching, and with respect to other disciplinary matters, the only assurance we have is that no change in Church discipline will destroy anything essential to the Church. Whether a change in discipline or whether a particular practical policy is or is not the best course of action is something that is not guaranteed by God to the Pope or to the bishops.

So, questioning strategy is not the same as questioning doctrine. When dissenters deny Catholic doctrine, they are challenging something whose truth has been guaranteed by the Holy Spirit. When loyal Catholics ask whether a particular strategy adopted by the bishops (or even by the Pope) is the best one, they are asking a very different question, a question whose truth is not guaranteed by the Holy Spirit and one that should be discussed within the Church. It is important to consider whether the policy of Pius or of Paul is the best one to follow in the present situation. We will never be sure of the answer unless we begin to ask the question.

Now to the second argument of the dissenters: When they challenge a Church doctrine or the authority of the Pope, is it true that they are doing what St. Paul himself did with respect to St. Peter? Again the answer is a definite no. As we shall see in a minute, what St. Paul questioned was the practical policy (the strategy) of St. Peter. He always supported the doctrines of the Church and Peter's authority on questions of faith and morals.

The best proof of St. Paul's attitude is to quote the Apostle himself. Here is what St. Paul writes in his Epistle to the Galatians about the importance of adhering to the Church teaching that has been handed down:

> I am astonished at the promptness with which you have turned away from the one who called you and have decided to follow a different version of the Gospel. Not that there can be more than one Gospel; it is merely that some troublemakers among you want to change the Gospel of Christ; and let me warn you that if anyone preaches a version of the Gospel different from the one we have already preached to you, whether it be ourselves or an angel from heaven, he is to be condemned. I am only repeating what we told you before: If anyone preaches a version of the Gospel different from the one you have already heard, he is to be condemned.

This is only one of many occasions when St. Paul (whose writings are part of the Bible and are inspired by the Holy Spirit) tells us how important it is for Christians to follow the traditional Church teaching. The Apostle goes so far as to say that if he himself were to deny Church teachings then nobody should pay attention to him even though he is an Apostle. He says further that if an angel from heaven challenges Church teachings we should pay no attention to the angel.

What did Paul mean by this last statement? He certainly knew that no angel from heaven would challenge Church teachings. If any angel did so, he would be from another place besides heaven.

It seems clear that what St. Paul means is this. If anyone with the prestige or brilliance or credentials of an angel from heaven, in short, anyone with the most impressive qualifications and personal talents, if such a person denies Church doctrines, then he is to be rejected and not to be followed. If St. Paul were writing today in this age of dissent, he might put it this way: If any theologian denies Church doctrines, even if he be a theologian with a hundred degrees who has published books that are read by millions; even if many hail him as the world's foremost "expert" on the teachings of Christ; even if he be the Rector of your diocesan seminary or the priest who runs the diocesan religious education program, then do not believe him but hold fast to what you have been taught.

In fact, St. Paul would not hesitate to go further and say that if the bishop himself were to challenge traditional Catholic teaching then the Catholics of his diocese should pay no attention to their bishop despite his position. After all, that is precisely what Paul did say when he emphasized to the Galatians that if Paul himself were to deny traditional Catholic teaching then they should regard him as condemned despite his position as an Apostle. If the Holy Spirit inspired the Apostle Paul to make such strong statements about doctrine, then what was the question on which St. Paul disagreed with St. Peter? The problem had to do with the way to deal with the Gentiles, i.e., those who were not Jews but wanted to enter the Church. Remember that Our Lord Himself had conducted His Mission only among the Jewish people. However, the Apostles had been sent forth to teach all nations. Therefore, they faced something of a new problem. As Jews, they themselves had followed the Jewish religious customs. Now they were preaching to Gentiles to whom many of these Jewish customs were foreign. Which traditions were essential to the religion established by Christ and which could be discarded?

Peter reached a doctrinal decision with which Paul heartily agreed. As opposed to others within the Church, Peter was sympathetic to the admission of Gentiles to the Church. In the Council of Jerusalem, the entire matter was discussed. By that time it was no longer a question of whether or not the Gentiles should be admitted, but of the terms. Did they or did they not have to observe the law of Moses? Peter settled the matter by deciding that they did not.

In making this decision, Peter ruled against a strong Judaistic movement in Jerusalem that had demanded that Gentile Christians should be circumcised and made to observe the Mosaic law. Paul was naturally happy with the outcome because he saw clearly the consequences of forcing non-necessary customs upon the Gentiles. It could split the Church into a Judeo-Christian section and a Gentile-Christian section. Rejecting this approach, the Council of Jerusalem, which was held around the year 49 or 50, decided under Peter's leadership that no burden should be laid upon the Gentile converts except for abstinence from meat offered to idols, from immorality, and from blood and meat containing blood. These three customs were kept by the early Church but other aspects of the Mosaic law were discarded. It should perhaps be noted also that what was involved was not only the doctrinal question of whether such customs were necessary, but a disciplinary question as well, namely whether, even if the customs are not essential, it is desirable to retain some of them. The Council did decide to retain a very small number of these customs, some of which could be discarded later when they were no longer considered to be desirable.

Paul supported both Peter's teaching and his authority. The problem that arose concerned a quite different matter, a practical judgment that Peter had made about the best strategy he himself should follow. It is uncertain whether the dispute that took place was either just before or after the Council, but a difficulty arose because of a change in Peter's way of acting. Peter had been associating freely with the Gentile members of the Church at Antioch until some of the Judaizers came from Jerusalem. Apparently in an attempt to avoid trouble, because Peter knew how upset the Judaizers were about the Gentile question and he feared that his association with Gentiles might further alienate these Judaizers, Peter avoided meeting with the Gentiles while the group of Judaizers were in town.

As one can imagine, this made the Gentiles feel hurt and wounded. Peter had ruled in their favor. He had been associating with them. Now he was avoiding them because he was sensitive to the feelings of the Judaizers. In such a situation, Paul, who was the champion of the Gentiles, objected to Peter's behavior. He pointed out publicly that Peter's action showed insensitivity toward the feelings of the Gentiles. In other words, the practical policy of Peter was having an effect that Peter did not realize and Paul wanted Peter to understand this. Paul's message is that Peter's practical policy, even though chosen for other reasons, seemed almost to create the impression that the Mosaic law was necessary after all, when the actual doctrinal decision had been exactly the opposite.

Application to Today

Once we understand the true situation involving Peter and Paul, is it not clear how applicable their discussion is for today? Paul was not challenging Church doctrine. To the contrary, we have seen how strongly he insists on it. He did consider it imperative, however, to question Peter's strategy because of the devastating effect it was having upon the Gentiles.

In today's Church, is there not a parallel with the decision of many in authority to tolerate dissent at least to the degree that they will not take any disciplinary action against Church dissenters? As the reason for Peter's practical policy was his concern for the feelings of the Judaizers, so the reason for the toleration of Church dissenters is often the concern for their feelings. Nevertheless, as the course of action adopted by Peter had the unintended effect of seriously hurting the Gentiles, so the apparent toleration of dissent in today's Church can have the unintended but very real effect of undermining the faith of many Catholics who believe strongly in Church doctrine.

Note that the Peter-Paul situation came about because, while the Judaizers were very vocal in making their feelings known, the Gentiles were not equally vocal (until Paul appeared on the scene and made Peter "sensitive" to the problem faced by the Gentiles). Similarly, in today's Church the dissenters are both vocal and effective in letting Church authorities know about their feelings. In contrast, loyal Catholics are often not as effective in communicating their "sensitivities" to Church authority. As Paul did not hesitate to speak up while still accepting both Church doctrine and Papal authority in order to urge Peter to change the practical policy he had adopted, so loyal Catholics today should not hesitate to speak up while still defending both Church doctrine and Papal authority in order to urge the present Church authorities to change the practical policies they have adopted.

When we see what actually happened, we realize that loyal Catholics who speak up are following a procedure that has been accepted from the beginning. They are the true descendants of St. Paul on this matter, and not the doctrinal dissenters who are so glib in citing St. Paul but who carefully avoid what he actually said about holding fast to traditional Church doctrine.

Of course, when we disagree on a matter of practical policy, we must always try to retain a reverence for Church authority itself. That is not an idle caution. It is remarkably easy to lose such reverence when one disagrees on a matter of strategy. Nevertheless, while taking care to retain the spirit of reverence, we should not be afraid to express our views. In God's Plan, we may have an insight that even those in authority do not have, as Paul had an insight that Peter, the first Pope, did not have until Paul brought it to him. We must work to make Church authority as sensitive to the needs of loyal Catholics as they are to the feelings of the dissenters. In a prayerful and Christian way, we must never cease to ask Church authorities to speak up in defense of the Faith.

11.
Strategy for Orthodox Catholics: The Net and the Cross

As we come to the end of this book, let us state once more that it has been written for Catholics who believe in the authority of the Pope and the teachings of the Church. As we indicated early in the book, such Catholics can be divided into two categories. First, there are those who have reverence for the Holy Father and Church teaching but who are not aware of the damage presently being done by the dissenters. The purpose of this book has been to inform them of the struggle going on within the Church so that they can act effectively in support of Church doctrine.

In the second category are those who already recognize the problem. With respect to this group, the purpose has been to set forth some of the strategies employed by the dissenters and to discuss how orthodox Catholics can best respond to these strategies.

To review, it is easy to understand why many orthodox Catholics are frustrated once we realize that the principal strategy employed by orthodox Catholics at present is to try to persuade the bishops to check dissent. In contrast, the principal strategy of the dissenters, at least of those whom we have described as "inside men," is not to push the bishops to action but simply to persuade them to remain silent. Thus, an essential goal for the future must be to develop an effective strategy for orthodox Catholics that does not depend upon action by the bishops, similar to the strategy of the dissenters. This does not mean that orthodox Catholics should abandon their effort with respect to the bishops. To the contrary, it is the suggestion of this book that both goals ought to be pursued, i.e., to do whatever possible to persuade the bishops to act against dissent but at the same time to develop

124

a plan of action for orthodox Catholics that will be effective even if the bishops do little or nothing.

In the next book, I will go into much more detail about specific activities that might be pursued by orthodox Catholics. Here let me simply say that one way to be effective is to look at the tactics of the dissenters already outlined in this book and, with respect to each of them, ask what loyal Catholics can do to keep the dissenters from reaching their goal. In some cases, it may also be possible to copy what the dissenters have done and to adapt it for loyal Catholics (although, in other cases, a tactic of the dissenters would be inappropriate for loyal Catholics.).

One thing is clear. It is vital for loyal Catholics to build their own "powerbase." Increasingly they must discuss how best to do this, and here is one area where orthodox Catholics have much to learn from observing the accomplishments of the dissenters. Remember that Our Lord Himself once held up the activity of the unjust steward as a model to be imitated by His followers, not insofar as the steward was unjust but insofar as he shrewdly looked ahead and used every opportunity to advance his position. Our Lord Himself told us to be "wise as serpents."

The activity of the dissenters also demonstrates how necessary it is to develop a "missionary program" to other Catholics. This "missionary program" of orthodox Catholics must stress the importance of Church doctrine and the authority of the Pope. In devising their plan of action, loyal Catholics must face such questions as these:

(1) How can we (like the dissenters have done on their side) put more and more orthodox Catholics in key positions where they will have an influence on religious education and communications? How can they be most effective once they get there?

(2) on the other hand, if one is not in a key position, what are some important things it is still possible to do?

(3) What should be our short-range and long-range strategy toward the bishops? How can we persuade them of the necessity to check dissent? Of the necessity to be personally active in promoting Church doctrine?

(4) What is the best way to reach out to the many Catholics who do support the Pope and Church teaching and involve them effectively in the struggle for orthodoxy? What training and assistance can we provide to these loyal "grass-roots" Catholics so that they can operate successfully in their parishes?

(5) What strategy should we employ to defend those loyal Catholics who are under attack by the dissenters?

We must study and respond creatively to all these questions to fulfill Our Lord's command to be "wise as serpents." But Jesus also gave us another command. At the same time He told us to be "wise as serpents," He also told us to be "innocent as doves." We must be *both* shrewd *and* reverent, an unusual combination and a difficult one to achieve.

This means that above all else, we must deepen our own spirituality. The effort to defend the Pope and Church doctrine requires our personal prayer and sacrifice. If we become bitter, we will lose the opportunity to act as Christ would want us to act.

That is another reason that support groups for loyal Catholics are so necessary. As a person naturally becomes angry and even bitter when cut off from those who support him, so loyal Catholics will find it almost impossible not to become bitter unless they build up groups among themselves in order to provide the necessary love and strength so that they can keep on praying and working and sacrificing, day by day, with determination and persistence, on behalf of the Holy Father and the teachings that have been handed down from Christ.

The Triumph of the Cross

There is perhaps one additional thing that should be said to loyal Catholics. One reason we may not have been as successful as the dissenters in planning strategy is that we can easily have an improper idea of what it means to trust in God. We can think to ourselves: This is God's Church; we know that the Church will survive no matter what we do (or fail to do); therefore, we do not have to worry about such things as human strategies, or support groups, or techniques of public relations, we just have to be spiritual and God will take care of the rest. If we have the right idea of "spiritual," that last sentence will be true. However, the preceding statements show that it is not the right idea of spiritual which is being put forth.

The truth is that God created man in a certain way. He gave us talents and He expects us to use these talents as best we can. While it is always possible for God to work a miracle, He usually prefers to work through us, and not only through us physically but through our planning and thought.

Remember the Gospel story of how the Apostles were fishing all night? Again and again they put down their nets but caught nothing. At Christ's command, however, they put their nets down once more. This time they caught an abundance of fish. Without Christ, their work was in vain. At the same time, Jesus wanted them to provide the human work of putting down the nets. In God's Plan, the Apostles had to do everything in their power before the miracle would be worked.

There most certainly is a necessity to trust in God. At the same time, we must follow the laws that He has laid down. Thus it is a law of human nature that support groups are necessary. That is the way Our Lord has created us. Remember Jesus Himself said that where two or three are gathered together in His Name, then He is in the midst of them. Therefore, it would be wrong for us to say that we do not need support groups, that we can rely on God alone. In God's Plan, we are not supposed to be such rugged individuals. Instead, we are supposed to work with others to build up the Body of Christ.

It is reported that Cardinal Cushing once attended a baseball game with a friend. One of the batters made the Sign of the Cross as he came to the plate. Cardinal Cushing's friend turned to him and asked: "Will that help him?" The Cardinal quickly responded: "It will—if he can hit." In other words, we must not expect God to supply for our own human effort. God works through us.

Of course, there may come a time when we have done all that we can and the outcome is beyond our power. Then we must trust God completely and allow Him to do whatever He wills with our work. Even if it seems that we have lost, we must still have faith. After all, Jesus appeared to have lost everything on Calvary, including life itself.

And that brings us again to the Cross. We considered it briefly in an earlier chapter. Let us meditate on the Cross once more and notice how all of us (the dissenters, Church authorities, and we ourselves) have an instinctive tendency to run away from it.

If we think about it, why do the dissenters revolt against Church authority? Is it not a desire to remove what might be referred to as the "theological cross?" The revolt against Church authority began in the Catholic academic world. It sprang from a strong desire to avoid a situation in which others (namely, the Pope and the bishops) could restrain their theological activities. That would be a cross. Behind the fine-sounding statement that "only our theological peers should judge us" is a determination to remove this cross.

And what about Church authorities, or at least those who value administrative calm so highly that they hesitate to take action against dissent. Is this not also a fear of the Cross? Most Church authorities recognize that if they stand up to the dissenters they will suffer much. It is abundantly clear that this has in fact happened to those bishops who have attempted to enforce Church doctrine and discipline. In contrast, those bishops who look the other way can avoid this Cross. How easy it must be to persuade oneself that the route which does not involve suffering is the right "pastoral" route to take.

But let us not be content to consider simply the dissenters or those in authority. What about us, the "grass-roots" Catholics who care strongly about Church doctrine? When we run away from the problem (for whatever reason); when we allow our nostalgia for the Church of the past to keep us from working as we should in the present; when we fail to realize that, for whatever reasons, it is in the present (and not in the past) that God has placed us; could we not also be running from the Cross? We talk about how wonderful the past was. When we make such a comment, is it not true that one of the things we are saying is that in the past other Catholics did things for us? Thus, it was not necessary for us to think about defending doctrine and discipline within the Church. The schools and the other Church institutions did that job. Now, although these institutions remain, we have to do it for ourselves. That means taking up the Cross.

We also avoid the Cross when we escape from the current Church crisis either by immersing ourselves in other matters or by finding an orthodox parish and hiding ourselves there so that we can be happy. Such a place, of course, is necessary in order to build an effective support system. But we cannot stay there all the time. We must also be missionaries who frequently leave the shelter of our home and go out into the stormy Church weather in order to fight for orthodox beliefs. If we do not go out, if we are content to stay within the support system that we have built, then we are escaping the Cross.

Finally, when loyal Catholics say that it is the Pope who must do it or the bishops who must do it, can this be yet another way to avoid assuming the responsibility for ourselves? Is this one more method of avoiding the Cross? If so, could our avoidance of the Cross be one reason the dissenters have succeeded so much, because we who believe strongly in Catholic doctrine hesitate to make the personal sacrifices that Jesus is asking of us, because we do not use our talents and abilities to the fullest (perhaps on account of the false idea that God will do everything for us)?

As we go forward to work for Church teaching, let us realize that it will not be easy. Perhaps we will be mocked even by those who ought to be supporting us. If that occurs, let us carefully check our own activity to see whether in some way we are not acting as we should to reflect the Light of Christ. But if, having looked at our actions honestly, we are convinced that the mockery is not our fault, then let us recall that Our Lord Himself was ridiculed frequently.

We can expect no better treatment than that accorded to Christ. It is a privilege to be like Him, and we are commanded to take up our cross and follow in His steps.